CALIFORNIA MISSIONS
History and Model Building Ideas
for Children

Edited by James Stevenson, Ph.D.

Published by
James Stevenson Publisher - California History
James Stevenson, PMB 109
1500 Oliver Road
Suite K-109
Fairfield, California 94533

Original Missions of California by Don J. Baxter
Compiled from a series of articles in *P.G. and E. PROGRESS*

This derivative work created with permission of P.G. &E.

Illustrations from work of Henry Chapman Ford
and Frederick V. Carpenter

David Graham provided Mission
Model Building Ideas

**California Missions History
and Model Building Ideas for Children**
is a derivative work,
Edited by James Stevenson, Ph.D.
All rights reserved by James Stevenson Publisher,
Copyright © November 1999
Created with permission of P. G. and E.

Missions of California
Original Copyright 1970
by Pacific Gas and Electric Company
San Francisco, CA

ISBN 1885852-13-4

Library of Congress Card Number: 99-069257

Contents

Illustrations

Preface

ONE BY ONE, in tents and brush huts on a hill beside San Diego Bay, the last of the conquistadors were dying. In the harbor close by, the two lonely ships that brought them there swung at anchor, their crews made smaller by an illness. The Spaniards were barely able to start Spain's last great colonial effort.

This story starts in May of 1769. For the 167 years before this time, the land that is now California was as hard to reach from the rest of the world as the surface of the moon. Its lands had been seen only from a distance by seamen on the treasure ships sailing in a great path which went from Manila to Acapulco in the Pacific Ocean.

But the world was changing and Spain was rushing to strengthen its claim to this fabled land. The Viceroy who governed Mexico was sending no marching armies, but only a handful of sandaled padres and a few soldiers to protect them in the wilderness. The story of this great adventure, and of the chain of missions they built, is the story of the founding of California.

In 1969 and 1970, California was looking back on these events during its 200 year anniversary celebration. To tell the story behind this Bicentennial was the purpose of this book, compiled from a series of articles in PG&E Progress as another public service by Pacific Gas and Electric Company.

We acknowledge with deep gratitude the assistance of many individuals who made this series possible. And most particularly do we thank the Rev. Maynard J. Geiger, O.F.M., whose review and advice contributed so much to the adequacy and accuracy of the original small history. James Stevenson Publisher has attempted to preserve the language of the original, while adapting it for children.

California Missions

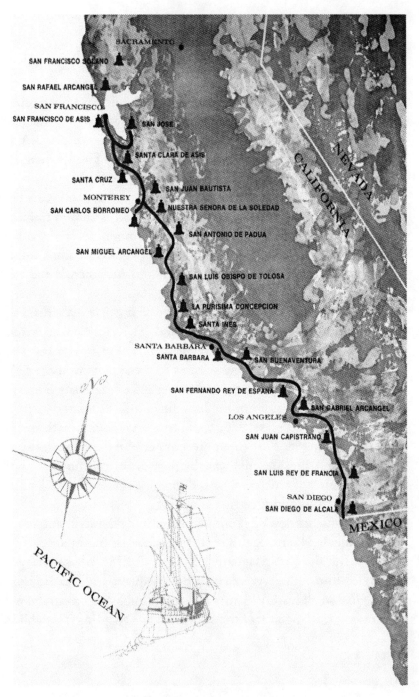

To Forge the Chain

An island of Amazons, a place of pearls and gold - this was a make-believe land called California dreamed up by a Spanish writer in 1510. Hernando Cortez, seeking more lands with gold to take, sent a group sailing westward in search of this story book island in 1533. His men found only the peninsula of Baja California and a few pearls in the oyster shells thrown away by the natives.

The first explorer to set foot in California itself was Juan Cabrillo, who anchored his two small vessels in San Diego harbor and stepped ashore at Point Loma on September 28, 1542. His ships went northward as far as Oregon but Cabrillo found only death and a lonely grave on San Miguel Island off Santa Barbara.

But the idea of great riches in California was still believed by many, even though a chain of Catholic missions established by Jesuit missionaries in Baja California proved it to be a poor desert land. In 1767 King Charles III of Spain ordered the Jesuits out of Baja California, partly because he felt that 16 surviving priests in the missions had been withholding pearls and gold due the royal treasury.

The man sent to Baja California to move the Jesuits was Don Gaspar de Portola, a middle-aged career soldier assigned to the lonely land. He was given the title of Governor of the Californias in stead of a promotion as a soldier. And the priest who took over the Jesuit chain of 14 missions was a 54-year-old Franciscan missionary named Junipero Serra. Behind Father Serra's gentle ways and slight stature was an iron will. He was determined to teach his Church's beliefs and to make a better life for the Indians.

The forced removal of the Jesuits brought Portola and Serra to Mexico's frontier at a time when Jose de Galvez, the king's inspector-general, was devising a grand plan to extend the frontier northward. In Portola and. Father Serra, Galvez saw the leaders for the group he would send out. He did not accompany them on their difficult journey.

The inspector-general wanted to extend the chain of missions northward to San Diego and Monterey to stop settlements in California by the British, Dutch or Russians. Russian fur trappers were sailing the north Pacific waters, opened up by the discoveries of Vitus Bering. The British dominated North America after defeating the French. Galvez persuaded King Charles that Spain was in a race against time to protect its empire, already coming apart at the seams.

For almost a year, Galvez labored feverishly at San Blas on the mainland and at Loreto on Baja California to outfit the brave group that would soon leave. He worked in his shirt sleeves beside priests and seamen, caulking ships and packing supplies for the missions which Father Serra would establish in Alta California.

The plan was for three ships and two overland parties to leave from Baja California points for a meeting in San Diego Bay, named and charted by Vizcaino. The ships had to push up the coast against winds which always blew from the northwest. The land parties had to blaze a trail through almost completely unknown country. The San Carlos sailed January 9, 1769, and the San Antonio on February 15. The San Jose sailed on June 16, had to put back once for repairs and a second time for water and finally sailed again in May of 1770. It was never heard from again.

The San Antonio reached San Diego on April 11. On April 29 the San Carlos was sighted, obviously in trouble, with two of its crew dead and most of the others sick.

The two ship captains looked southward for help from the overland party being led by Portola and Father Serra. But the first of this group was still picking its way through the deserts of Baja California. Galvez's race against time was turning into an even grimmer race than he had feared.

The first explorers to enter California by foot or horseback had to struggle through the wild and barren land that had been unexplored for centuries.

On March 24, 1769, Good Friday, the first band of Spain's settlers left the Indian village of Velicata bound for San Diego harbor, about 350 difficult miles to the north. Leading it were Capt. Fernando Rivera y Moncada. He had been a garrison commander on the peninsula for 20 years. Father Juan Crespi, close friend and helper of Father Serra was also in the group. With them were twenty-five cavalrymen, some one hundred fifty pack mules, three mule drivers and about fifty mission Indians.

They faced thirst, hunger and cold every step of their journey. Five of the Indians died and about thirty deserted. Their supply of beef jerky gave out before the end of the journey and they had only a cup of chocolate and one tortilla a day: "without any seasoning or sauce," complained Father Crespi later.

The party followed Indian trails "abounding in stones and thorns." Sometimes they used a navigation tool called an "astrolabe" and as they neared San Diego they were guided by friendly Indians.

On May 13, fifty-one days after leaving Velicata, they saw - in great excitement - the San Diego harbor and the main masts of the San Carlos which had arrived two weeks earlier, and the San Antonio which had arrived a month earlier. But when the land and sea parties came within sight of each other the next day their cheers and joy soon faded.

Rivera and Father Crespi were shocked to find that 21 sailors and several soldiers from the ships had already died and, of the entire sea group, only about a dozen men were still on their feet. For their part, the earlier arrivals learned that Rivera's party had almost no food left to share and, in fact, had to be supplied from their own slender stores.

The two groups had fulfilled part of their mission - to reach San Diego. But now it was impossible to continue on to Monterey. The newcomers helped move the camp to a better site on a high hillside, where the ship's doctor, Don Pedro Pratt, could take better care of the sick although he himself was seriously ill. Then they began to unload the San Antonio so it could sail back to San Blas for help.

Meanwhile, Portola and Father Serra, with 10 soldiers and

Sgt. Jose Ortega as a scout, had set out from Velicata on the same day the first unit had reached San Diego. A pack train was loaded with foods and cattle Portola regretfully took from the poor missions. Indians, mule drivers and two servants made up the rest of the caravan.

Before leaving, Father Serra had founded a mission in Velicata and left Fray Miguel de la Campa in charge. With Rivera's trail to follow, Portola's party made better time, although some days marches lasted just an hour and a half because of the problems they had as Ortega rode ahead to hunt for the trail signs and to each side to search for food, water and camp sites. Father Serra himself almost delayed the caravan. For 30 years he had suffered with an ulcerated leg, said to be the result of an infected mosquito bite. Now his leg was so painful and swollen he couldn't walk, but a cure used on mules relieved the pain and enabled him to resume the march.

A little before noon on July 1, Father Serra and his party reached the little settlement on what is now called Presidio Hill above San Diego harbor. There he wrote, "I met all who had set out before me, whether by sea or by land; except those who were dead."

And the dead were many. About 60 of the 159 persons who had reached San Diego were dead of scurvy, and many others were sick. On July 9 the San Antonio sailed for San Blas with reports of the explorers' plight. The ship had a crew of only eight. Two were alive when it arrived at San Blas.

Portola felt he must continue to Monterey. He offered Captain Vicente Vila of the San Carlos 16 soldiers as a crew to help him sail northward in search of the beautiful port described by Sebastian Vizcaino 167 years before. But Vila had only a single experienced sailor and a cook who were still alive, of all his seamen. He refused Portola's offer.

It was decided, then, that Vila and the San Carlos would stay behind in hopes the supply ship San Jose would appear. Fathers Crespi and Francisco Gomez would go with Portola and establish a mission at Monterey, Fathers Serra, Juan Vizcaino and

Fernando Parron would stay in San Diego.

On July 14, 1769, Portola and most of the surviving soldiers and officers headed north from San Diego. And in the silence they left behind, Father Serra, surrounded by a handful of soldiers, his two priests and the ailing seamen, raised a cross on the side of Presidio Hill two days later. Then he sang a High Mass, preached a sermon and formally founded Mission San Diego de Alcala. By a slender thread, California was formally tied to Spain.

The Search for Monterey

While Father Serra and his sick companions remained behind to establish a mission beside the San Diego Bay, Don Gaspar de Portola had gone in search of Monterey.

Sebastian Vizcaino had stepped ashore there in 1602, but Spain, busy with other parts of her great empire, did not get around to claiming this very important port until 167 years had slipped by. Now the Russians were on the horizon and Spain at long last was moving.

On July 14, 1769, a long column of soldiers and pack animals headed up the coast from San Diego. Riding ahead were Sgt. Jose Ortega and his scouts. Then came Portola and his staff: Lt. Pedro Fages, engineer Miguel Costanso, Franciscan missionary fathers Juan Crespi and Francisco Gomez, six soldiers and some Indians who would build the bridges and help clear the trail for the pack train which followed next. Bringing up the rear were Capt. Don Fernando Rivera y Moncada, more soldiers and more Indians driving spare mules and horses.

There were 63 men in all. The arrival of these beings from another world, riding strange animals, were greeted with curiosity. Indians would come from miles around to sit and stare at the white men as they made camp until Portola would lose his temper and send them away. Neighboring villages would often try to outdo one another in offering hospitality to these mostly bearded and leather-jacketed white men, giving them seeds, nuts and fish to eat. Near what is now Ventura the explorers were kept awake by the mournful wail of whistles with which the natives serenaded them during the night.

For their part, the Spanish were equally interested in the wondrous land which no white man had ever explored before. They were shaken by earthquakes beside the Santa Ana River and again in the Los Angeles basin. They marveled at the bubbling tar pits of La Brea and at streams which flowed at night but dried up during the heat of the day. Far to the north, they encountered giant red-woods, larger than any trees they had ever known, and huge "deer" with great branching horns which actually were elk.

Keeping as close to the shoreline as possible, their train could make only about 7 to 10 miles on a good day. Until they reached the Los Angeles River basin, they followed roughly along the line of the present Highway 101, but kept further inland to avoid the marshes and deep ravines along the beach.

Scouts came to the ocean again at what is now Santa Monica, but were turned back by the Santa Monica Mountains which went right down to the water. So the caravan picked its way through Sepulveda Canyon, crossed the mountains to the Santa Clara River Valley and followed it back to the sea at Ventura. From there, Portola's men followed the present route of the highway as far as Gaviota Pass. Instead of turning inland, they kept to the coast around Point Conception.

Portola's party passed into the San Luis Obispo Valley. There they saw a great number of bears and succeeded in killing two, although one of the wounded grizzlies injured two mules and almost got their riders before he was finally slain.

Continuing northward, the explorers passed Morro Rock and within a few days found their progress blocked beyond San Simeon by the towering Santa Lucia Mountains rising out of the ocean.

Turning to the east through land too rough, "not only to the men, but even to goats and deer," in the words of Costanso, the men followed a route scouted by Captain Rivera. They finally entered the Salinas Valley near what is now King City. From there it was an easy road to where the river empties into Monterey Bay, where they arrived on September 30, two and a half months after leaving San Diego.

But neither Portola nor anyone else could recognize the great open roadway as the sheltered harbor described by Vizcaino. Thinking they had overshot their mark - they were already above the latitude given for the port - Portola sent scouts around the "Point of

Pines" (Monterey Peninsula). There they saw only the small Carmel Bay and the Santa Lucia Mountains in the background.

Very confused, Portola called a meeting. It was decided that Monterey must still lie to the north, and though 17 of the men were weak and ill with scurvy, they should press on. They left Monterey, not knowing they were destined to discover another great port.

The Discovery Of San Francisco Bay

Ayala entering San Francisco Bay

Sixty-three men, "skeletons spared by scurvy, hunger and thirst," headed their worn-out horses northward on a cold and foggy October morning in 1769. They were resuming their search for Monterey Bay for although they had camped by its shores for five days, Portola and his explorers had not recognized it.

The decision to push on was a grim one. Many men had been deathly ill for months from their poor diet and scurvy. They had to be tied onto their horses. Provisions were short; the weather was turning bad. The fear of death by sickness and starvation rode with them as they struggled across the steep ravines that cut the seaward side of the Santa Cruz Mountains.

A storm drenched them to the skin at Ano Nuevo Beach but strangely it seemed to improve the health of the sick, easing their swollen joints and firming their loose teeth. Then, on October 31, in bright sunshine, the explorers crossed a ridge on Montara Peak and saw the coastline forming a great arc to the northwest. Portola looked at some sailing charts, and was sure that they were looking at the Farallone Islands, the distant headland of Point Reyes and the curve of seacoast the maps would call San Francisco Bay.

This, Portola decided, meant that Monterey was to the south; that somehow the soldiers and missionaries had missed the "fine harbor" the king of Spain had instructed them to find and settle.

Not all agreed with this conclusion, however, so Portola set up camp where the city of Pacifica is now and sent Sgt. Ortega and his scouts ahead with orders to return within three days. They left on November 1, following the beach and probably turning inland without sighting the Golden Gate. Topping a rise, they were astounded to see a great inland bay spread out below them. A vast harbor unknown to the world.

Evidence suggests that Sir Francis Drake, 190 years earlier, had sailed his Golden Hinde at least near the port. He was said to have posted a plate of brass claiming the land for Queen Elizabeth. But if he did, the details and importance of Drake's find were kept secret; Portola's men had made a great discovery for Spain.

The next day, while Ortega was still exploring, a small party of hunters also saw the bay and returned to camp with this startling news. The following evening the scouts came back with their report on the bay and on an even more exciting development: Indians had indicated by signs that only two days march away was a port with a vessel in it. Could it mean that Monterey and the long-overdue supply ship San Jose were still to the north?

On November 4 the entire Portola group set out in search of the port. They rode up the beach a short distance, turned eastward to follow a ridge to the summit of the mountains. There, on a site known today as Sweeney Ridge, the entire group now gazed down on the great harbor. Father Juan Crespi called it "this most notable estuary" and suggested in a letter that if the port of Monterey should not be found, "we have in place of it this fine bay of San Francisco, in which to set up the standard of the Holy Cross."

At the foot of the mountains, Portola camped at what is now Palo Alto on November 6 and sent Ortega ahead to look for the hard-to-find port and ship. He returned in four days "very downcast:" the report of a ship was mistaken; the Indians were hostile; there was another very large arm of the bay to the northeast that would have to be skirted. He and his scouts had turned back near what is now Hayward.

By ballot, the officers and missionaries voted to retrace their steps and search again for Monterey which they now knew lay behind them. Living on geese - and finally on pelicans and seagulls - the explorers again followed the shoreline of the bay they didn't recognize and pitched camp on the south shore of Carmel Bay. From November 29 to December 9 they scouted the coastlines to the north and south but found nothing which looked like the fine harbor described by Vizcaino. "Is it possible to think that it has been filled up, or destroyed in the course of time?" wondered Miguel Costanso, the group's engineer and map maker.

Very short of food and forced to kill their mules for food (which few soldiers could eat at first), the group voted to return. But first a big cross was erected on the beach, with an inscription cut in the wood which said: "Dig! At the foot thou wilt find a writing." A report was of their failed search was buried there.

On January 24, 1770, after more than six months of travel, the group neared San Diego. They had not found the port of Monterey, they had seen no sign of the supply ships that were to meet with them, they had had no word from San Diego. Would Father Junipero Serra and his priests and tiny group still be alive? Was there still a Mission San Diego de Alcala?

In the words of Costanso: "All of us were returning with misgiving lest the settlement had become a place of solitude."

San Diego de Alcala

Mission San Diego de Alcala

Things had not gone well for Father Junipero Serra and the handful who had remained at San Diego.

They had erected a cross on Presidio Hill on July 16, 1769 and dedicated a crude brush chapel as Mission San Diego de Alcala. But the Indians remained unfriendly. They watched the soldiers bedridden with scurvy and the new graves being dug and finally, on August 15, fell on the settlement.

The Indians were driven off, but not before several defenders were wounded and a servant boy slain. Troubles piled higher. Food supplies were very low. Nineteen more men had died from scurvy by the time Portola returned and reported that he had not been able to find Monterey. "You have come from Rome without seeing the Pope," remarked Serra sadly, realizing from Portola's description that he had reached Monterey Bay without recognizing it.

With no food, many sick or dead, and hostile Indians, the situation was very bad. Don Gaspar announced that the settlement at San Diego would have to be abandoned if a supply ship did not arrive by St. Joseph's Day, March 19.

The brave Father Serra determined to remain behind if necessary. Meanwhile he ordered nine days of prayer for the appearance of a supply ship. The novena was to end the day the ship was due, but the morning of St. Joseph's Day passed with no sign of a vessel.

Then, at three in the afternoon, sails appeared on the horizon. It was the San Antonio, laden with supplies and bound for Monterey where Portola was to have been. Though the ship sailed out of sight, Portola agreed to wait a while before departing. Four days later, the San Antonio reappeared - it had lost an anchor and had turned back to get one at San Diego. The mission was saved.

Plans were made to push on to Monterey and start a second mission and presidio in New California as ordered. Serra sailed aboard the San Antonio and Portola led a second land group both arriving without incident within eight days of each other. It was a grand triumph that set church bells pealing throughout Mexico City when the news arrived.

But at Mission San Diego, Fathers Fernando Parron and Francisco Gomez, protected only by Sgt. Ortega and a few soldiers, worked hard, but got little help from the Indians. More trouble between the soldiers and Indians would slow the missionaries efforts to convert. By March 1771, hunger again caused talk of giving up. Then the San Antonio luckily appeared again. This time with supplies from Mexico and ten Franciscan fathers to staff the other missions to be founded in California.

In August of 1774 the mission was moved to its present site, six miles up the valley of the San Diego River. A church of wooden poles roofed with tiles was built, together with other rooms, workshops and storage buildings. More Indian families were converted to Christianity and the small settlement was beginning to prosper. But beneath the surface all was far from calm. Indians were angered by soldiers molesting Indian women, "neophytes," Indian converts, resented punishment for breaking white men's rules. The tribes were more and more upset over the Spanish settlement in their territory.

About one o'clock in the morning of November 5, 1775,

more than six hundred Indians surrounded the mission, took everything from the church and set fire to the buildings. Those inside took refuge in the cook-house, using bales of clothing to hade from the arrows and firebrands.

All the rest of that long night, two unwounded soldiers held off the circling attackers. Father Vicente Fuster stood holding a large bag of gunpowder while fiery remains of the blazing roof fell around their heads. "That night seemed as long as the pains of purgatory," wrote Father Fuster later. "We were all longing for daylight."

When dawn finally came, Father Fuster and the handful of defenders were left amid nothing but ruins, while out in the fields lay the body of Father Luis Jayme. He apparently had walked bravely out to the angry Indians, expecting the neophytes to not harm him.

The missionaries returned to the valley site in July of 1776, and a temporary church was finished by October. In 1780 a more spacious and substantial church was erected, with thick adobe walls and beams of pine and poplar. The interior was elegantly finished by Indian artisans.

After the early 1780's, the years passed in peace and prosperity. By 1797 San Diego was the most populous of all the missions, with 1,405 neophytes, a school, a flourishing vineyard and an irrigation system. In September 1808 the present church was begun and it was completed in 1813.

But time for the Franciscan missions was fast running out. Mexico was to gain its independence from Spain in 1821 and a law taking the missions away from the Catholic Church was passed in 1833. This is called "secularizing" the missions.

In 1834 the San Diego Mission was transferred from the authority of the Franciscan fathers to a government administrator. By January of 1842 a visiting Frenchman was to write, "The buildings and church are in ruins…the ranchos now belong to private parties who have (taken them over.)" The official end of Mission San Diego de Alcala came on June 8, 1846, when the mission and 58,000 acres of land were granted free to Don Santiago Arguello by Governor Pio Pico.

After the Mexican War, the mission buildings were used as barracks in which American troops lived. In 1862 some 22 acres of land and the ruined mission itself were returned to the Catholic Church by the U.S. Land Commission. A move to rebuild the church began in 1891 with a drive to round up bells for the distinctive bell tower, only the base of which was left. Restoration work speeded up in 1931, and today the mission appears much as it did a century and more ago. It serves as a parish church, a peaceful reminder of another era, standing on a hillside overlooking the freeway and modern-day Mission Valley.

San Carlos Borromeo de Carmelo

Mission San Carlos Borromeo de Carmelo

It was Pentecost Sunday, June 3, 1770. Under a spreading oak on the shore of sparkling Monterey Bay, Father Junipero Serra formally founded Mission San Carlos Borromeo and Don Gaspar de Portola claimed Alta California for Spain.

Cannon fire from the tiny transport San Antonio, instead of choir and sacred music foretold of the conflict between the missionaries of the church and the soldiers and officers of the state that would eventually cause problems for both institutions.

But whatever lay ahead, that Sunday morning was an important occasion. They had failed once to recognize Monterey Bay, but now Portola's party returned by land and by sea to worship under the oak where explorer Sebastian Vizcaino had knelt 168 years earlier. Governor Portola, having secured a new empire for Spain, turned his command over to young Don Pedro Fages and sailed for Mexico and out of the pages of California history.

Five hundred miles away the priests and soldiers at San Diego were facing hunger and hostile Indians. But at Monterey the natives were friendly, language barriers were soon overcome and the converts helped to secure food and build shelters. There was a reason.

When Portola and Father Juan Crespi had camped beside Carmel Bay on their first search for Monterey, they had left behind a large wooden cross with a message at its base. At night, the Indians said, the lonely monument was bathed in a heavenly light and at times seemed to grow so that it almost touched the sky. This explained the offerings which the explorers found when they returned to the site and also explained the ready respect the Indians had for the cross and the men who wore it.

Troubles with Fages and the soldiers helped prompt Father Serra to move the mission to its present site beside Carmel Bay, where there was more water, farmland and Indians. The cross was raised there August 24, 1771, and the first buildings were completed in December. Relations with Fages worsened and in 1772 the aging Serra made the long and difficult trip to Mexico City and persuaded the viceroy to relieve Fages.

The next viceroy proved equally troublesome and the Spanish and Mexican governors that followed, with a few notable exceptions, cared little for the missionaries work and tried to turn it to their own ends.

In 1774 Juan Bautista de Anza broke an overland route to Monterey from Sonora. He arrived again on March 10, 1776, leading more than 240 settlers through the pouring rain. Most of them were bound for the mission and presidio to be founded at San Francisco.

With artists and craftsmen to train the Indians and with supplies more easily available, the missions flourished. In 1781 a larger church was completed at Carmel and a fifth, a sturdy adobe structure, took its place in 1783.

On New Year's Day, 1782, Father Juan Crespi died at Carmel and was buried in the chapel. A grieving Father Serra felt that his own end was near. He made a final inspection trip of his beloved missions - by then numbering nine - frequently weeping at the plight of the poor Indians living in villages where the mission system had not reached. On August 27, 1784, Father Serra walked to the church of San Carlos to receive the last sacraments. Father Francisco Palou, tears rolling down his face, read the service for the dying. The following afternoon Father Serra passed away quietly in his sleep in his tiny cell at the age of 70. He was buried beside his old companion, Father Crespi, while cannon at the presidio and aboard ships in the bay were fired as a sign of respect.

The missions were entering their golden age as first Father Palou and later Father Fermin Lasuen took over as president. The cornerstone of the present stone church at Carmel was laid in 1793 and, under the directions of master stone mason Esteban Ruiz, the beautiful Moorish building rose skyward. It was dedicated in 1797.

Mission San Carlos continued to do well even as trouble swirled around it. In 1803 the flu hit the mission and killed at least 86 Indians and hundreds of others fled to the hills. In 1814 the beautiful vaulted stone roof had to be replaced because of earthquake damage. The waves of the Hidalgo Revolution in Mexico began to break upon the shores of Monterey and supplies again became difficult to obtain. In 1818, Hippolyte Bouchard and Peter Corney, sailing against Spain in two ships under the Argentine flag, sacked Monterey for six days and the mission's resources went to aid those left homeless and to rebuild the city.

By 1819 Father-Presidente Vicente Sarria was struggling to keep the mission in repair. News of Mexico's independence reached Monterey in 1822 and from then on the missionaries had trouble with the anti-church governors. The missions taken from the church in 1834 and were later auctioned off, one by one. San Carlos was in such ruins by 1846 that when Governor Pio Pico planned to sell it there was nothing left of value. In 1852 the roof crashed in. It is said that the famous bandit Joaquin Murieta hid in the ruins when wounded.

The mission property was returned to the church in 1859 by the United States and efforts at restoration were begun in 1882 when the bodies of Fathers Serra, Crespi, Lasuen and Julian Lopez were exhumed and reinterred in the same vaults. This act helped focus attention on the ruins at Carmel and funds began to flow in.

A wooden roof was placed on the church which, though it saved the structure, marred its lines. This roof was replaced with the present tile roof during an era of rebuilding which began in 1931 and still continued in 1970.

Today Mission San Carlos Borromeo del Rio Carmelo is again a place of worship, designed as a basilica by Pope John XXIII. Its courtyard and vaulted chapel, its sheltered corridors and waving palm trees all present a picture of the mission as it was in the height of its prosperity when colorful religious processions alternated with fiestas and when peace and contentment, for all too brief a while, reigned supreme.

San Antonio de Padua

Mission San Antonio de Padua

By the middle of 1771 the Spanish were worried about keeping control of Alta California. For two years the Franciscan missionaries and soldiers had braved this land - kept going by hope and ingenuity, not by the long and uncertain supply line from Mexico.

By May 1771, a mission and presidio had been established at both San Diego and Monterey. In each place the buildings were enclosed by a stockade and made of poles driven in the ground and plastered over with mud. They were roofed with tule stalks.

For the third mission in his projected chain, Father Junipero Serra chose a site in a beautiful oak-dotted valley in the Santa Lucia Mountains. About 60 miles southeast of Monterey, it was on the route that Portola had blazed on his trek between San Diego and Monterey.

Near present-day Jolon, Father Serra hung a bell on the limb of an oak and rang it with such force that he surprised his companions. But the sound echoing through the lonely Valley of the Oaks brought a lone Indian to the camp to watch as Father Serra on July 14, 1771, dedicated Mission San Antonio de Padua. Welcomed by the aging padre, the native left to bring back others of his tribe. It was the start of a long and happy relationship between Indians and priests.

Father Serra remained for about two weeks while work began on the rude shelters. Then he returned to Monterey, leaving behind Fathers Miguel Pieras and Buenaventura Sitjar and a small band of soldiers, sailors and Baja California Indians. They finished the crude buildings, planted grain and began learning to converse with the natives.

A little later an aged woman came to the mission asking to be baptized. She said her father had told her about a robed man who, on four occasions long ago, had appeared from the sky to talk about Christianity. Missionaries had been startled to find Indian legends from the Southwest where, 150 years earlier the Indians seemed to have already learned a great deal about the church. Investigating, the priests heard of a nun in Spain who claimed she and others had made many supernatural visits with the Indians and who offered amazingly accurate descriptions of places and events.

Another explanation of the Indian legend is offered by the Mormon Church. Mormons believe that it was Jesus Christ who came to the American Indian to minister to them.

No explanation of the phenomenon was ever officially accepted by the Catholic Church, but the California missionaries frankly wondered if some mystery did not lie behind the unusual friendliness of the Indians at San Antonio (and later Santa Cruz, where a similar legend of a robed visitor existed among the Indians).

The missionaries had trouble with their own soldiers. Capt. Pedro Fages, the military commander, stopped at San Antonio and replaced a band of hardworking soldiers with a lazy troop of idlers who harassed the Indians. Nevertheless the mission continued to do well, even with early crop failures.

Although a regular church had been completed in 1772,

work was started on another one at the present site in 1773 because it was closer to a dependable source of water. There began a building program which helped the mission grow into one of the richest in the chain, with many people living near it.

A new church was started in 1779 and finished the following year. Before his death, Father Serra made a tour of the missions and spent the last days of 1783 with Fathers Pieras and Sitjar. None had worked harder or given him less grief than these two priests from his native Majorca. They had baptized 1,127 Indians since Serra had first rung the bell, and had built the finest church in California, except for Santa Clara.

As the mission prospered, a large wing with rooms for the growing number of Indian converts was added in 1790. Skilled craftsmen, or the priests themselves, taught the natives skills intended to make them self-sufficient eventually. Granaries were built and in 1806 a unique waterpower flour mill (since restored) ground the grain for which San Antonio was famous.

In 1810 the present church was started by Fathers Pedro Cabot and Juan Bautista Sancho. Built of adobe with a facade of clay brick, it stood on a rock foundation 10 feet deep. The church was completed in 1813.

Building activities continued until 1829, despite crippling levies made on the missions by the Mexican government. When the missions were taken from the church in 1834, the one priest at San Antonio was relegated to a back room by the government administrator who moved in and took over.

A visitor to San Antonio in 1841 found Father Jose Gutierrez paralyzed and without necessities which were withheld by a former helper, by then the administrator. A handful of Indians huddled in roofless dwellings nearby.

Father Gutierrez left in 1844 and when Governor Pio Pico offered to sell the plundered mission the following year there were no takers. When the United States won California from Mexico the mission with a plot of land was restored to the church, but there was no way to keep it going.

In 1903 efforts were started on restoration by the California Landmarks Commission, but the work that was completed was ruined by the 1906 earthquake. Work continued slowly, and the present reconstruction largely got its impetus from a grant made in 1948 by the William Randolph Hearst Foundation.

Today Mission San Antonio de Padua is again a place of worship for families in the valley and a place of retreat for Franciscan padres. Its pleasant pastoral setting and its red-roofed buildings make the traveler think he has stepped back in time. But the empty irrigation ditches and the rubble of the once-thriving work area surrounding the mission show clearly that here, too, time has taken its toll.

San Gabriel Arcangel

Mission San Gabriel Arcangel

San Gabriel Arcangel was the anvil on which much of California was forged. This was the role of Mission San Gabriel Arcangel. And like an anvil, the great stone walls of its church still stand, though softened by the hammer of time.

San Gabriel was the fourth in Father Junipero Serra's chain of California missions. It was the end of the trail from Sonora, Mexico, the goal of those who dared to make "the journey of death" across the desert to California. This mission was the parent of the pueblo of Los Angeles, its padres hosted the first American fur traders and its pleasant surroundings beckoned thousands of emigrants from the States.

San Gabriel was founded on September 8, 1771, by Fathers Angel Somera and Pedro Cambon. Exploring the plain below the San Gabriel Mountains, the Franciscans selected a site in what is now Montebello. There, beneath a canopy of branches, Mass was celebrated. The next day the first rude buildings were started by the priests and soldiers, the Indians helping in the work.

Harmony with the Indians was interrupted, however, by a soldier who insulted a chief's wife and who slew the Indian when he attempted to get revenge. By taking quick conciliatory action, the Spanish eventually restored good relations with the Indians.

Except for this incident, San Gabriel flourished from the start. The troublesome soldiers were replaced by others who helped build a new church and warehouse. The mission crops and live-stock thrived.

Then, in October 1773, Sebastian Tarabal, a Baja Indian, struck out for home by going eastward across the desert. It was a fortunate defection. Tarabal arrived at the frontier village of Tubac, Sonora, just as Juan Bautista de Anza was preparing to find an over-land route to Monterey. Although Tarabal had lost his wife and child in the terrible desert crossing, he agreed to retrace his steps and guide Anza's historic group. On March 22, 1774, Anza's small group rode into Mission San Gabriel. He had opened a great road to Mexico and California's future no longer depended on the peril-ous sea voyage from Baja California.

Anza returned to San Gabriel on January 4, 1776, with two hundred-forty settlers bound for the new mission and presidio to be established at San Francisco. He found the cattle fat and fields fertile at San Gabriel Mission, which had been moved about five miles northwest to its present site in May, 1775. But he also found that the cooking of the Indian neophytes was very different from what he was used to, and not to his taste, even though he was a hardened frontiersman.

In 1780, Governor Felipe de Neve dispatched Capt. Fernando Rivera y Moncada, a veteran of Portola's group, to Mexico to recruit soldiers and settlers for the pueblo that de Neve would establish at Los Angeles. They reached San Gabriel safely but Rivera did not.

He and his men stayed behind to rest the cattle near two pueblos de Neve had established on the Colorado River. They died in an Indian uprising, as did some fifty townspeople and four missionaries, including Father Francisco Garces, the explorer-priest who had helped Anza blaze his trail.

Despite this bad beginning, and in the face of opposition from Father Serra, de Neve went ahead with the founding of Los Angeles. On August 26, 1781, the settlers left San Gabriel Mission and took up homesteads on lands assigned to them in the pueblo about nine miles to the northwest.

Although friction between the colonists and the Indians and missionaries developed as Serra feared, Mission San Gabriel continued to prosper. By 1790, it was second only to Mission San Antonio in the number of neophytes; in farm products it outstripped all the rest.

It became the spiritual and cultural center of the growing Los Angeles area. The mission had ranchos surrounding it at various distances. Its farming and manufacturing efforts were so successful that in 1830 the mission even had a shipyard. The 99-ton schooner Guadalupe was built there, then taken apart and hauled to San Pedro and launched. It sailed for San Blas, loaded with mission goods.

About 1791 the foundations of the present church were laid. The four and one-fourth foot thick walls, supported by great buttresses, are of stone to the high windows; from there burned brick was used to support the vaulted roof. The church was dedicated in 1805, but an earthquake in 1808 caused the arched roof to be replaced with a flat one and another quake in 1812 toppled the bell tower.

When Jedediah Smith and his band of rough looking trappers entered California in 1826, guided there by two runaway Indians, they stayed at the mission for two months. Their leader's face bore the awful scars of a mauling by a grizzly bear. But though their presence upset Mexican authorities, the populace treated the Americans so well that several deserted Smith for the peaceful, happy life of early California.

But that life was already changing. The fertile mission lands were a prize for the taking and in 1834 the government secularized the missions. At San Gabriel, Father Tomas Estenaga wrote of the host of people who moved in and ate up mission supplies. He fled to Sonora in 1835 with Father Francisco Ibarra of San Fernando, but returned later when the missions were briefly returned to the Franciscans. He found that everything of value had been taken.

The Franciscans left for the last time in 1853 long after Governor Pico's plan to sell the mission buildings was prevented by the arrival of U.S. troops.

San Gabriel mission's church continued to be used through the ensuing years by secular clergy. In 1908 the church was again put in charge of a missionary order the Claretian Fathers, who began the slow process of restoring some of the workshops, gardens and buildings that stood beside the church in two great quadrangles. Today, in its pleasant garden surrounded by ruins, graves and ancient walls, stands a sun dial whose Latin legend reads: "Every hour wounds - the last one kills."

San Luis Obispo de Tolosa

Mission San Luis Obispo de Tolosa

Like an old soldier reminiscing in the sun, Mission San Luis Obispo sits on a hill in the center of the pleasant community that grew up around it. Relics of past greatness and memories of bitter humiliations are preserved within the adobe walls of this fifth California mission founded by Father Serra.

Early in the 19th Century, travelers on El Camino Real saw the quadrangle of mission buildings set like a jewel in a valley ringed by hills. White adobe walls and red tiled roofs contrasted with the foliage of fig and olive trees. Irrigation ditches glinted in the cultivated fields; an aura of reverence and industry hung like a benediction over this favored place.

But a few years later the mission buildings, their gentle inhabitants driven out, echoed to shouts of rabble. Bandits ruled the streets of the pueblo and one despairing citizen wrote American Governor Mason that "the whole place has for a long time been a complete sink of lawlessness."

The story of the mission began in 1769 when Don Gaspar de Portola and Father Juan Crespi passed that way in their search for Monterey. They noted the pleasant valley just a few miles from the ocean with its friendly Indians - and a great many bears.

The Spaniards were drawn there again in 1772 - first to hunt bears when starvation threatened the new mission at Monterey and later to found Mission San Luis Obispo de Tolosa. Father Serra, on his way from Monterey to San Diego to meet two supply ships, arrived in the Valley of the Bears on August 19, 1772. Upon the present site, he raised the cross and dedicated the new mission September 1. Then he rode off to San Diego, leaving behind a single priest - Father Joseph Cavaller - and five soldiers, two neophytes and a few supplies.

From this simple beginning, the mission rose relatively quickly to prosperity and prominence. Aided by Indians the priests replaced the temporary wood pole buildings with adobe ones. They taught agriculture and mechanical arts to the growing number of Indian converts. After renegade natives fired the thatched roofs of the mission buildings on three occasions, a priest found a way to make roof tiles. This was not their first appearance on a California mission, however. Father Serra, writing to Father Fermin Lasuen, credits Mission San Antonio with being the first to make and use the tiles. In modern California, tile roofs with the "Mission look" remain popular.

The present church was completed in 1793 and most of the priest's quarters - now a museum - were finished in 1794. Then, in 1798, came Father Luis Martinez, a jovial, brave and outspoken priest who for more than 30 years guided the destinies of San Luis. The mission gained a reputation for richness that went a bit beyond its actual prosperity.

Walter Colton, American Alcalde at Monterey, credited the mission with ten times as much livestock as was ever recorded in the padres careful ledgers. The ruins of old furnaces in Arroyo Grande gave rise to a legend of secret silver mines; more likely they were but the ruins of lime kilns. Regardless, Father Luis dispensed hospitality with an open hand and gave clothing and money to support the poor, hard-pressed soldiers of Spain and later of Mexico.

When Argentine rebels attacked the California coast in 1818, Father Luis rose from a sickbed to lead a troop of neophytes to do battle at Santa Barbara. Failing to engage the enemy there, he marched down the coast as far as San Juan Capistrano, wishing in vain for two cannon and a chance to fight the rebels.

He had little use for the bureaucrats who, far removed from the slender restraints of the government in Mexico City, were methodically undermining the mission system. His caustic letters were finally stilled in 1830 by an old foe, Governor Jose Echeandia, who had Father Martinez arrested on a charge of treason. He was given an illegal court-martial and hastily banished to Spain.

Mission San Luis Obispo was secularized in 1835 and its lands parceled out. The last Franciscan missionary was Father Ramon Abella, who lived in increasing poverty in the crumbling mission while whiskey traders from Santa Fe grew rich. Finally, broken in health and with no more Indians left to minister to, he retired to Mission La Purisima in 1841. He was succeeded by Father Jose Gomez, the first secular priest ordained in California.

In 1845, Governor Pico sold the remaining mission buildings for $500, although Father Gomez was permitted to retain several rooms for living quarters. Title to the mission was restored to the church by the United States after it acquired California in the war of 1846.

Meanwhile in the dark years following the war, the good citizens of San Luis Obispo lived in fear of the bandits who roamed the area freely. Joaquin Murieta and his men took over the town for several days in 1853, camping in the mission garden and sleeping in what was later Sinsheimer's store. But the slaying of Murieta later that year by Harry Love's Rangers, the formation of a vigilante committee and the establishment of stage lines out of San Luis helped to restore order.

Father Garcia had made efforts to restore the mission and its gardens as early as 1847. In 1880 the crumbling arcade along the front of the mission was torn down, the buildings were en-closed in clapboard to protect them and a wooden cupola was added. While this detracted from the appearance, it preserved the mission so it could continue to serve the spiritual needs of the parish, as it still is doing today.

Serious restoration efforts began in 1935 and today the courtyard, church and priest's quarters appear much as they did a century and a half ago. Not a trace remains of the other two sides of the mission quadrangle, where once stood a hospital, workshops and living quarters for the Christian Indians.

San Francisco de Asis

Mission San Francisco de Asis

A small adobe church and a tiny cemetery packed with historic headstones, makes up Mission San Francisco de Asis today. Its modest appearance gives little hint of the incredible efforts that led to its founding, nor of the influence that Mission Dolores, as it is better known, had on California history.

Spanish treasure galleons from the Philippines were part of the story of the naming of San Francisco Bay. In 1595 Sebastian Cermeno, exploring the coast for places where the galleons could put in on their way to Mexico, was shipwrecked at Pt. Reyes. He and his 70 men built and sailed a tiny open boat down the coast to Mexico.

The name that he gave his starting place, the Bay of San Francisco, was preserved for future map makers. Almost two centuries later Father Junipero Serra, packing for his group to California with Don Gaspar de Portola, was told that the first missions he was to establish would be San Diego, San Carlos and San Buenaventura. The inspector-general joked with the Franciscan missionary: "If St. Francis wants a mission, let him cause his port to be discovered." And perhaps he did.

For, oddly enough, neither Portola nor any of his men recognized Monterey Bay where San Carlos was to be. Instead, they pushed north and stumbled upon the great landlocked bay of San Francisco on November 4, 1769. When word of the discovery reached Mexico City - together with the news that on the second try Monterey had been found and settled - the government directed that a mission and presidio be built at San Francisco.

With supplies and manpower scarce, the priests and soldiers in distant California were unable to comply. Missions San Antonio and San Gabriel were established reasonably close to Monterey and San Diego. In March of 1772 Don Pedro Fages and Father Juan Crespi surveyed the eastern shore of San Francisco Bay, but the mission moved no closer to reality.

Later that year Father Serra founded Mission San Luis Obispo - fifth in the chain and last for almost four years. Serra had to make a long and almost fatal journey (he fell grievously ill) to Mexico City to iron out supply problems and to have the troublesome Fages removed as military governor.

Capt. Fernando Rivera, Fages successor, was equally difficult. But prodded by an impatient viceroy, Rivera led a troop of soldiers through driving rains and bitter winds to seek a site for a settlement at San Francisco. He and Father Francisco Palou planted a cross beside the Golden Gate - the first white men to stand there.

In 1772 Juan Bautista de Anza had blazed an overland trail to Monterey. Now Viceroy Bucareli, moving to forestall the advancing Russians and English, ordered Anza to lead a train of settlers to San Francisco. At the same time he instructed Rivera to take possession of the port. And in March of 1775 he dispatched the transport San Carlos, under Juan Manuel de Ayala, from San Blas with orders to explore San Francisco harbor and rendezvous with Anza's party.

Early in August 1775 the San Carlos cautiously sailed through the Gate. This was the first ship to enter the bay - or the second, if Sir Francis Drake preceded Ayala. For 40 days Ayala's men explored the bay from a base at Angel Island. Then they sailed away after leaving letters for Anza at the foot of the cross Rivera had erected. As for Rivera, he had chosen to ignore the viceroy and San Francisco was still unoccupied.

Meanwhile, Anza was recruiting settlers from among the poor in Sonora. Offering generous bounties, rations and clothing, he enlisted 240 persons, including soldiers and their families. Many were of African or Indian descent - all were willing to brave the 1600 mile trip.

The settlers, with 590 horses and mules and 355 head of cattle, left Sonora on October 23, 1775. They arrived, weary and gaunt from cold and hunger, at San Gabriel on January 4. Delayed there by an Indian uprising at San Diego, the colonists finally reached Monterey in the pouring rain on March 10. It was a triumphant arrival that quickly soured.

The unpredictable Rivera had left word that the colonists were to remain at Monterey, although food was scarce and housing almost nonexistent. Angered, Anza led a small party to explore San Francisco anyway. Standing atop a white cliff at the entrance to the Golden Gate, Anza and his men watched young whales blowing water from their spouts and a line of dolphins frolicking in the blue ocean. Father Pedro Font, Anza's chaplain, wrote: "I do believe that if populated as in Europe, there would be nothing more pretty in the world, for this place has the best accommodations for founding on it a most beautiful city."

The following day, March 29, Anza' party came upon a lovely creek emptying into a lagoon. The hollow was fragrant with wild flowers - a fine site for a mission, Father Font decided. The place was named Arroyo de Nuestra Senora de los Dolores.

Anza returned to Monterey and took tearful farewell of the colonists, whom he placed under the charge of his lieutenant, Jose Joaquin Moraga. Then he rode off on the long trail back to Sonora, his mission finished.

On the way he met Captain Rivera heading north. The two officers passed each other coldly. Anza was to become governor of New Mexico, Rivera was to be relieved as governor of California and to die in a battle with the Indians on the Colorado River - in a vain attempt to keep open the trail that Anza had pioneered.

Excitement ruled Monterey on June 3, 1776, when the historic packet boat San Carlos sailed into the harbor. Built in the primitive shipyards of San Blas, Mexico, she and the smaller San Antonio had carried members of the Portola group to the unexplored shores of California in 1769. Since then she had weathered many a stormy passage, exploring the coast and carrying men and supplies from Mexico to the missions.

Now she had arrived to load and transport to San Francisco the belongings of the settlers who were to establish a presidio and mission. The arrival of the San Carlos signaled the end of the delay which had kept the settlers chafing for months at Monterey after their trek from Sonora.

Two weeks later 17 soldiers and seven colonists - with wives and children - rode northward out of Monterey, led by Lt. Moraga. Although Governor Rivera had authorized the founding of a presidio only, Father Serra sent Fathers Francisco Palou and Pedro Cambon along as chaplains. Ten Christian Indians driving pack mules and almost 300 head of cattle made it an impressive train.

On June 27 they arrived at the Arroyo de las Dolores which Anza and Father Font had selected for a mission site three months earlier. They put up a camp of 15 tents, erected an arbor as a temporary chapel and on June 29, 1776, Font celebrated Mass.

While the colonists waited in the rain for the San Carlos, the missionaries explored their new home. They found the Indians went naked except for capes of otter skins and pelican feathers - when the weather got too cold they would smear themselves with mud; the women wore big grass skirts.

After a month, Moraga moved the colonists to the site of the presidio, but Father Palou and his assistants remained behind to cut and transport timber to the mission site, which was about 400 yards east of the present mission. On August 18 the San Carlos, which had been blown clear back to San Diego, finally sailed into the harbor. Aided by the sailors, the crude shelters at the presidio and mission rose rapidly.

Ceremonies officially dedicating the mission were held October 9. Firecrackers and rockets fired from shore were answered by the guns aboard the San Carlos and two of the beef cattle were barbecued.

Far more than the ramshackle presidio, whose buildings were always deteriorating faster than the indolent soldiers could repair them, Mission San Francisco de Asis - or Dolores as it is better known - nailed down Spain's claim to Northern California. On April 25, 1782, Father Palou laid the cornerstone of a second and larger chapel built, like the first which it replaced, of poles driven in the ground and plastered with clay. The following year - 1783 - he laid the foundations of the present church and completed work on a temporary chapel at the new site, freeing the original site for agriculture.

Within the mission compound, Indians began making adobe brick and, in 1788, work began on the present church. It was dedicated August 2, 1791.

There were sorrows for Mission Dolores almost from the beginning. Governor Philippe de Neve refused to provide supplies; a rancho had to be started in 1785 in what is now San Mateo to supplement the crops at San Francisco. Neophytes were ravaged by measles and other white men's diseases.

As the fledgling town of Yerba Buena grew up around the mission compound, settlers became the increasingly interested in the valuable mission lands. Mission Dolores was one of the first to feel the effects of secularization: a civil commission was appointed to take it over in 1834. By 1841 the extensive mission buildings were falling to pieces through neglect. The property was restored to the church after the United States acquired California in 1846 and the mission grew again in importance as a parish church in the brawling, booming gold rush city of San Francisco.

The mission church withstood the great quake of 1906 and it stands today much as it did in its heyday. Its thick adobe walls and its roof timbers and tiles are original. The ceiling still shows the decorations by the Indians and many of the sculptured figures of the mission' patron saints are the work of neophytes.

On one side of the church is a small graveyard in which much of San Francisco's history is recorded in stone. Here are the graves of James Casey and Charles Cora, hanged by the Vigilantes in 1856. Here also is buried William Leidesdorff, a black man who was an early civic leader, American vice-consul, chairman of the city's first school board, hotel man and owner of the first steamboat ever to operate on San Francisco Bay. Lt. Moraga is buried there, and a plaque honors the memory of Father Palou, first priest at the mission, president of the missions after Father Serra's death and noted historian and biographer of Serra.

In the small mission church, religious services are held twice yearly (on Memorial Day and on June 29 - the anniversary of its first Mass). But on its other side rises the great basilica which was completed in 1918, replacing an earlier church built in 1876 and wrecked by the earthquake. And around both buildings swirls the busy metropolis of San Francisco, symbol of an empire built - not by force of arms - but by the persuasive ideas of a small group of men of peace.

San Juan Capistrano

Mission San Juan Capistrano

Beautiful even in ruins, Mission San Juan Capistrano today is still the "Jewel of the Missions." A ruined sanctuary, all that remains of the great stone church, rises serenely above fragrant gardens, ivy softening its rugged outline. Ancient adobe walls soak up the few sounds of civilization that filter through the trees and the long arched corridors of the restored mission buildings are quiet pathways to another age.

The many legends add to the romantic setting. Stories have attached themselves to the mission: of swallows who return on St. Joseph's Day every year, of the bells that rang by themselves to announce the death of an Indian maiden, of star-crossed lovers buried when the church collapsed and of buried treasure guarded by a ghostly flame.

But the calm of today was not always a feature of San Juan Capistrano. It was founded first on October 30, 1775, by Father Fermin Lasuen at a site Father Junipero Serra had chosen on the road between San Diego and San Gabriel. Eight days later news of an Indian uprising forced the padres and soldiers to bury the heavy church bells and retreat to the safety of the presidio at San Diego.

A year was to pass before Father Serra himself returned to found the mission a second time. The bells were dug up and hung from a branch and on November 1, 1776, San Juan Capistrano became the seventh mission in the chain.

Work began at once on a crude chapel made of poles plastered with mud. By the end of 1777, an adobe church had replaced this temporary structure and Father Serra returned to officiate at ceremonies in this chapel in 1778 and 1783. Enlarged in 1785, the chapel is there today - the only one still standing in California in which Father Serra is known to have celebrated Mass.

The Indians were friendly and readily took to instruction in religion, farming and various trades. Streets of adobe houses grew up around the mission as the neophytes helped develop Capistrano into a growing community and, being close to the ocean, a center of trading with Yankee ships. By 1795 the old adobe chapel was too small and Father Vicente Fuster planned a huge stone building which would be the most outstanding building in the whole mission chain.

Its cornerstone was laid in 1797 and for nine years the priests and Indians worked to build the great church. Using chains and oxcarts, they dragged and carried boulders from the river beds, quarried limestone form the hills and cemented the rocks and stone into walls seven feet thick. It was completed in 1806 and on the steeple above its great ceiling stood a golden rooster that could be seen flashing in the sun from many miles away. The fiesta that followed the church's dedication was remembered for many years.

Only six years later the beautiful church lay in ruins. On December 8, 1812, an earthquake sent most of the church crashing down and 40 Indians at early morning Mass were killed. The padres did not have the heart to rebuild. They cleaned up some of the rubble and returned to Serra's old chapel.

In 1818 the Argentine raider Hippolyte Bouchard attacked Monterey and stopped to plunder San Juan Capistrano. But his men were driven off after a day by a troop of Indians, led by Father Luis Martinez of Mission San Luis Obispo, and others.

But the mission's days were numbered. Mexican Governor Jose Echeandia arrived in 1825 to enforce the "order of secularization" which turned the churches over to priests not of the Franciscan order. Lands were supposed to go to the Indians. This had

Mission San Juan Capistrano

always been the long-range goal of the Franciscans, but Echeandia's decrees were unplanned for and created chaos - especially at San Juan Capistrano.

Neophytes, whose lives had been changed from the days when they lived on tribal lands, had not been prepared for independent living in the new culture, and many gambled or drank away their properties, often resorting to robbery in order to survive. By 1829, Alfred Robinson described San Juan Capistrano as a "lonely, dilapidated mission, once the grandest structure of its kind in California."

   When Governor Figueroa chose the mission as the site of a pueblo of free Indians in 1833, mission activity was all but ended. Despite efforts of a few priests who stayed on, Indian lands gravitated into the hands of the settlers. In 1845 Governor Pico sold the mission to his brother-in-law and a partner for $710 - a sale that was not allowed when American troops captured California the following year.

   Some efforts at rebuilding were made, but a gale blew away most improvements. The mission moldered away until 1895 when Charles Lummis and his Landmarks Club raised money and did much to halt the decay. In 1910 an ailing priest, Father John O'Sullivan, arrived in the hamlet of San Juan Capistrano. Intrigued by the ruins, he obtained permission to become the parish priest and with the help of the townspeople - some of them descendents of Indian neophytes - started extensive restoration efforts. These have culminated in the beautiful mission gardens and ancient adobe buildings which, with the ruins of the great stone church, make up San Juan Capistrano today.

Santa Clara de Asis

Mission Santa Clara de Asis

Barricaded inside Mission Santa Clara de Asis, 175 American men, women and children prepared for battle. The big wooden gates in the wall were jammed shut with trunks of trees and as night fell every man who could handle a weapon was on guard duty. In the crumbling belfry of the old church, a lookout peered northward into the darkness, while nearby in a field of mustard 32 armed men huddled in wait for the advancing horsemen of Don Francisco Sanchez.

It was the winter of 1846; the war with Mexico was nearing its end. Col. John C. Fremont and his battalion had marched off for Los Angeles, leaving their families at Mission Santa Clara. It was on this mission that Don Francisco was descending, planning on revenge for the attack on his rancho by the Americanos.

After a tense and fearful night, the battle, when it came, was minor. There was much fighting, but the only death was an American killed when his field gun blew up. The British consul arranged a truce.

The original Mission Santa Clara was to have been situated near what is now the town of Castaic in Los Angeles County. But

Spain, eyeing Russian activity in North America, ordered that priority be given to two new missions and a fort on San Francisco Bay.

Thus Mission San Francisco was founded October 9, 1776. On January 12, 1777, Mission Santa Clara was established by Father Tomas de la Pena, using the name and supplies that had been destined for Castaic.

The site, crossed frequently by Spanish explorers since the days of Portola's group in 1769, was on a fertile plain - populated with many Indian villages - beside the Guadalupe River at the southern end of the bay. While six Christian Indians from Baja California cut logs and poles for the buildings, Father Jose Antonio Murguia was bringing supplies and church goods from Monterey.

By year's end the missionaries had a church and dwellings, two corrals, a bridge, a dam, irrigation ditches - and neighbors. For on November 7, 1777, Lt. Jose Joaquin Moraga, who escorted the missionaries and soldiers to Santa Clara, returned from San Francisco with nine soldiers and five colonists and their families to found the pueblo of San Jose, the first town in California.

A disastrous flood demolished the mission on January 23, 1779. Father Pena and the neophytes moved to higher ground while Father Murguia remained in mud and rain to guard supplies. When the weather improved, a second temporary mission was built.

Santa Clara Mission prospered and on November 19, 1781, Father Junipero Serra laid the cornerstone for a permanent adobe church. In a niche he placed some coins, medals and a cross. They were dug up 130 years later by a crew laying a gas main.

The new church was the most elaborate of all then existing in Serra's chain. It was dedicated May 15, 1784 - but Father Murguia, who had labored so hard to build it, died four days before the ceremonies. The 70-year-old Father Serra presided, but time was running out for him also; he died three months later.

Santa Clara entered a period of great prosperity. For 35 years its destinies were guided by two remarkable men: Father Magin Catala, a gentle and holy man, and Father Jose Viader, an athletic outdoorsman.

Both were men of action: Father Magin, upset by the riotous living of the residents of San Jose, cleared a four mile boulevard straight to the church door and planted three rows of black willow trees along it - the famous Alameda. Father Jose, once attacked by three toughs, won out so convincingly that their leader, Marcello, became a convert and close friend of the priest.

In 1812, the great California quake which shattered so many of the missions, did severe damage to the adobe structures of Santa Clara. The fathers were still repairing the damage in 1818 when another ruinous temblor convinced them to move again. The fourth and present site was chosen. A temporary church was erected and used until the permanent one was completed in 1825. The present structure is a faithful copy of this church.

Santa Clara was one of the last of the missions to be secularized, but it went downhill quickly after a civil administrator took over in 1836. By 1843 Father Mercado was trying to get General Mariano Vallejo to return 4,000 sheep which he had taken - for services to the government. His successor, Father Jose Real, sustained himself and the mission by renting rooms.

Long a center of education - including being the site of the first English language school in California - the mission was turned over to the Jesuits in 1851 for a school. After four years of financial struggles, the school started by Father John Nobili was recognized as a college - and today's Santa Clara University is the second oldest university in the state.

The crumbling mission chapel was rebuilt in 1862. The old church was eventually replaced by two wooden churches, but each was destroyed by fire. The present church was dedicated October 12, 1929. While it contains very little of the original building, an adjacent museum houses many artifacts from the days of glory that once surrounded Mission Santa Clara.

San Buenaventura

Mission San Buenaventura

Where the muddy Colorado River rolled by, was the memory of violent death in the smoldering ruins of two California desert missions. There, in the summer of 1781, the Yuma Indians had risen in anger to slay half a hundred settlers and soldiers and to crumble one corner of a tottering empire.

Among the dead were two old California hands: Captain Fernando Rivera, who had marched with Portola, and Fray Francisco Garces, Franciscan priest and explorer who had blazed the desert road to California with de Anza. The tragedy on the Colorado was a grim reminder that beneath the placid surface of mission life lurked the constant danger of sudden violence.

This lesson was not lost along the coast of California where Father Serra's growing chain of missions had stalled at eight. First the military, fearful of an Indian uprising, had been against founding more missions. Then there had been opposition by the missionaries to a new government policy that would make all new missions part of a program of bringing Spanish settlers into Indian

51

territory - a policy responsible for the desert disaster.

So it was not until five years after the founding of Mission Santa Clara that Father Serra was able to establish Mission San Buenaventura. Situated on a narrow neck of coastline beside the Santa Barbara Channel, it was his ninth and last. He could build it on traditional lines because Governor Felipe de Neve, who recognized the need for this strategic and long-delayed mission, was faced with a refusal by the Franciscans to send missionaries unless the traditional purpose was followed.

Mission San Buenaventura was founded on March 31, 1782 - Easter Sunday - by Fathers Serra and Pedro Cambon. Work started at once on a temporary chapel and living quarters close to the mouth of the Ventura River. This chapel was soon replaced by a permanent adobe church. From the start, the mission flourished. The Chumash Indians were numerous, friendly and exceedingly skillful: they fished the ocean in well-built canoes and their women wove baskets so tight they would hold water.

A reservoir and aqueduct system seven miles long was built to bring water to the mission grain fields. Tropical plants and fruits flourished in the mild weather so that the variety of produce from the mission was astounding. By 1794 the typical mission quadrangle of apartments, dormitories, artisan's shops and garden had been completed except for the permanent church.

After almost 15 years, the present church of stone, brick and adobe was dedicated September 9-10, 1809. In the great earthquakes of December, 1812, the structure was badly damaged and it required two more years of effort to make it serviceable again.

A chapel near Casitas called Santa Gertrudis - remnants of which were uncovered in recent years - became a refuge in the winter of 1818 when Hippolyte Bouchard, pirate and rebel, was pillaging the coast. For more than three weeks the mission population huddled in the hills, with the church furnishings hidden in caves, under brush or buried in the ground. Violence surfaced again the following year when a party of 22 Mojave Indians visited the mission. A frightened sentry tried to detain the Mojaves and a fight ensued in which 10 Indians and two soldiers were slain. The Mojaves fled, but for months the mission lived in fear of reprisals by war parties.

The social and political revolution in Mexico further disrupted the work of the missionaries. Many Indian neophytes grew angry at working to support the growing numbers of lazy soldiers and of "settlers" who were only too willing to live by the labor of the Indians. Land grabbers and hordes of petty officials bedeviled the padres who were worn out and ill defending their charges.

"My cart will soon be coming for me across the rocky waste," wrote the dying Father Jose Senan in 1823. His successor at San Buenaventura, Father Francisco Senan, complained: "Here I am, further along in years than was the deceased, taking over the reins of this ministry (already half in ruins), probably because I was born to be a sort of a stopgap."

The mission was secularized in 1836 and though it was blessed with an honest administrator, the inevitable decline set in. In March 1836, a two-day battle was fought over the mission by the troops of rival contenders for governor, adding more damage to the crumbling mission buildings.

On June 18, 1846, the mission and its lands were sold by Governor Pico to Don Jose Arnaz for $12,000. Arnaz was perhaps California's first real estate promoter, for he subdivided the town into lots and advertised them for sale - or even free, under certain conditions - to Americans in the East. Fortunately he got no takers, for the sale was held illegal by the United States and the lands were restored to the church.

With only a few interruptions, services have been held almost daily in the present church since its dedication in 1809. An earthquake in 1857 tumbled in its tiled roof and a well-meaning parish priest "modernized" the structure late in the last century. However, San Buenaventura has been restored to its original state - although almost all traces of its auxiliary buildings vanished as the growing commercial center of Ventura moved closer to the sturdy old mission.

Santa Barbara

Mission Santa Barbara

Towering above the palm trees on a rocky point
near the Pacific Ocean is the great stone church of Santa Barbara,
"Queen of the Missions." It stands in a vast amphitheater formed
by the Santa Ynez Mountains and the curving coastline, a natural
stage whereon much of California's history has been enacted.

The two tiny caravelles of Cabrillo were the first to anchor
in the bay there in 1542. Vizcaino, in 1602, was the one who
entered the name "Santa Barbara" on a sailing chart. And from the
day Portola and the Franciscan missionaries first rode into the area
in 1769, Santa Barbara was highly regarded as a mission site.

But it took Father Junipero Serra 13 years to win official
approval for a mission at Santa Barbara. When he arrived there in
1782, he happily assisted in founding a presidio and chapel, only to
be told by Governor de Neve that the mission must wait, although
he himself had proposed a mission there.

Serra returned sadly to Monterey, where he died two years
later. It was his successor as Father-Presidente, Fermin Lasuen, who
finally founded the mission on December 4, 1786. Santa Barbara

was the tenth in the chain and it rose to prominence in a period of prosperity to be known as the "Golden Age" of California's missions.

The temporary church was of the usual wooden poles, but it had an adobe front and a red tile roof. This was promptly replaced by a larger adobe edifice in 1789. And by 1794 an even bigger adobe church stood on the hill, while around it the usual mission quadrangle of buildings was taking shape. This church, enlarged and refined through the years, stood until the great earthquake of December 21, 1812, when it was badly damaged. Repaired, it was used for worship while the present imposing church of stone was erected around it.

The majestic structure was built under the direction of Father Antonio Ripoll. From 1815 to 1820, blocks of native sandstone were quarried and laid into walls that were as much as 51/2 feet thick. The facade was that of a Greek temple, flanked oddly but harmoniously by two Spanish bell towers, only one of which was completed at the church dedication in 1820.

During the two day dedication fiesta, food and drink were dispensed lavishly. Fireworks and rockets painted the night skies, musicians strolled the streets and soldiers and administrators paraded in elegant plumage. There was bull-baiting and dancing and the fountains by the mission sparkled with a myriad reflected lights.

This was the high point in the mission's history. Two years later news of Mexican independence reached California and a growing social unrest was accelerated. In 1818 Californians had weathered the attempts of Argentine rebel Hippolyte Bouchard to plunder their towns and spread revolt. At Santa Barbara, Bouchard sailed away without landing when confronted with a presidio guard reinforced by 150 mission Indians that had been armed, outfitted and drilled by Father Ripoll.

But in the spring of 1824, Indians at three missions revolted against the increasing cruelty of the soldiers. At Santa Barbara they armed themselves and wounded four soldiers in a tussle over the weapons. The reprisals by the troops were so severe that the neophytes fled to the interior. Only after two the visit of two groups and the personal plea of Father Commissary-Prefect Vicente de Sarria and Father Ripoll could they be persuaded to return.

Dissension grew in the pueblos and presidios. In 1828 the soldiers at Monterey went on strike, as it were, for pay. Not higher pay, just pay of any kind. Again, in 1829, the garrison openly revolted, chose a rancher and ex-convict named Joaquin Solis as its commander, and marched southward to battle Governor Jose Maria Echeandia at Santa Barbara on January 13, 1830. The loyalists held the presidio and mission. After two days of exchanging shots from great distances, the rebels retreated and scattered.

The great days of the mission were fast drawing to a close. In 1834 Santa Barbara was secularized, but Narcisco Duran, then Presidente of the missions, moved his headquarters there. This, and the fact that Francisco Garcia Diego, first bishop of California, chose Santa Barbara as his seat, prevented the pillage that ruined so many other missions.

Then in 1846 both of these men died within a month of each other. The ever-ready Governor Pico moved in to sell the mission, excluding the church, for $7,500 - a sale promptly annulled by the arrival of United States troops.

In the ensuing years, Santa Barbara became the site of a college for training Franciscan novices. In 1899 St. Anthony's Seminary was completed on land once part of the mission quadrangle.

The great stone church, which had been painstakingly replastered in 1886, was badly shattered by an earthquake in 1925. The facade and the east tower were rebuilt or repaired during the next two years - but this work had to be done all over again in 1950-53 because of structural defects.

La Purisima Concepcion

Mission La Purisima Concepcion

Mission La Purisima Concepcion stands in the pleasant Santa Ines Valley not far from Lompoc, the second mission of that name to be built by the Franciscans in California. The first was established on the Colorado River in 1780; it and a nearby mission were wiped out by Yuma Indians the following year.

La Purisima was founded on December 8, 1787, by Father Fermin Lasuen. He erected a large cross on a site in what is now the town of Lompoc and then retired to Mission Santa Barbara to await the end of the rains.

Building began in the spring of 1788 and by the end of that year a chapel and other buildings of wood poles and adobe had been built. Eleventh of the 21 coastal missions, La Purisima was favored by fertile soil and friendly Indians - but droughts kept the mission poor until the padres developed an elaborate irrigation system.

By 1798 the mission had outgrown its small church and the priests laid out the foundations for a larger one. However, they had no master builder nor the money to hire one, so construction languished until about 1800. By the end of 1802 the church had been finished and the big mission garden enclosed by an adobe wall. By 1804 there were more than 1,500 neophytes living there.

On the morning of December 8, 1812 - the 25th anniversary of its founding - La Purisima was rocked by the first of a series of earthquakes. On December 21 a great quake lasting four minutes leveled much of the mission and rain completed the devastation by turning the adobe ruins to mud.

Fathers Mariano Payeras and Antonio Ripoll did not give up. They moved across the river to the present location and started over. Temporary structures were put up and a new and more elaborate irrigation system was built - even though the padres were receiving no more financial aid from Mexico and the struggling mission had to help support the soldiery.

In 1815 Father Payeras was named president of the missions and La Purisima became his headquarters. In 1818 the wooden palisade interior of the temporary church collapsed and work on a new church was commenced on the same site. This church was dedicated in 1825.

Worn out by his labors, Father Payeras died at his mission in 1823. The following year the Indians at neighboring Santa Ines revolted against the cruelty of the soldiers. The revolt spread to La Purisima, where the Indians seized the mission after slaying a neophyte and four unlucky travelers on the road. They permitted one padre and the mission guard to leave, then turned the church into a fort.

For almost a month they held the mission. A force of more than 100 soldiers tried to regain the mission but it was Father Antonio Rodriguez who persuaded them to surrender. Seven ringleaders were executed and 12 imprisoned.

La Purisima tried to return to normal, but its days were numbered. Ten years later it was secularized and a series of corrupt administrators quickly disposed of much of the land and cattle that remained. By 1829 there were only 122 Indians left at the crumbling

Mission La Purisima Concepcion

mission, most of them ill and in need.

In 1845 La Purisima was sold by Governor Pico to John Temple of Los Angeles for $1,110 for the buildings and 15,000 acres of land. Thereafter the property passed from owner to owner and the decaying buildings were used as barns and stables. In 1874 title to a few parcels of land and the ruined buildings was returned to the church, but so complete was the desolation that most of the land was sold off.

In 1912 an attempt was made to start restoration of La Purisima. But little was done until the 1930's when the state collected 940 acres into one holding and the Civilian Conservation Corps started rebuilding.

First the adobe structures, then the elaborate water system

and finally the beautiful gardens were rebuilt in as authentic detail as possible. It was dedicated on December 7, 1941, the same morning as Japan's attack on Pearl Harbor. Today Mission La Purisima Concepcion stands much as it did a century and a half ago, when it was a flourishing farming community and an important stopping point for travelers on El Camino Real. It is now a State Historical Monument - and still a stopping place for travelers.

Santa Cruz

Mission Santa Cruz

Few new missions had such a pleasant setting or such a promising beginning as Santa Cruz, twelfth in the growing chain of Franciscan missions in early California.

Founded in 1791, Mission Santa Cruz stood on a rise not far from where the San Lorenzo River flows into the great Bay of Monterey. The fertile land was rich in grasses and berries; game was plentiful. Forests of pine and redwood covered the mountains, the Indians were friendly and an aura of good will existed, temporarily at least, between the missionaries and the civil authorities in California.

Father Fermin de Lasuen, successor to Junipero Serra as head of the missions, raised the cross at Santa Cruz on August 28. On September 24, 1791, the two padres assigned to the mission and an escort of soldiers arrived at the site. The next day Mass was said and the mission formally founded while the local Indians watched.

The temporary buildings, made of poles and slabs of split redwood, took shape rapidly but the onset of the rainy season proved that the mission was too close to the river. So on February 27, 1793, the cornerstone of a new church was laid on higher ground.

It had a stone front, stone foundations on which rested adobe walls five feet thick and was topped by a tile roof.

The new church was dedicated May 10, 1794. Later that year the British explorer Captain George Vancouver visited the mission to buy produce for his two ships and presented the padres with ironwork for a gristmill. By 1796 the mill was in operation, two sides of the mission quadrangle had been completed and the mission population had reached 523 neophytes. From that point on, the fortunes of Mission Santa Cruz were all downhill.

In 1796 Governor Diego Borica founded California's third pueblo, which he called Branciforte, across the river from the mission. The first settlers were shipped there from San Blas, many of them troublemakers who had been given their choice of jail or California. To swell the population, soldiers whose enlistments were up were induced by offers of land and money to settle there.

The settlement effort was not a success, and its failure dragged down the mission too. Many of the settlers were more interested in visiting at San Jose than in farming. When told to stay at Santa Cruz, they harassed the Indians. Some 200 neophytes fled Mission Santa Cruz in the next two years.

In 1798 rain and high winds lashed the mission buildings and the following year floods did more damage. The padres repaired the church, making slight alterations to its design. But they were unable to do much about the settlers usurping mission lands or the fact that there were only 30 or 40 neophytes left to sustain the mission.

Things were to get worse. In 1812 Father Andres Quintana was murdered by a group of Indians who several years later were captured and imprisoned.

In 1818 the ships of Argentine rebel Hippolyte Bouchard sailed into Monterey Bay and the mission residents fled to safety. Bouchard sacked Monterey, but he turned away from Santa Cruz. However the residents of Branciforte proved to be no better than the pirate. Recruited to "save" the valuables of the church, they responded so enthusiastically in taking the churches treasures, that

Father Ramon Olbes indignantly refused for a while to return to his looted mission.

In the years that followed, Branciforte became a haven for adventurers and smugglers. The first Americans arrived and with them came sawmills and saloons - and fighting between the Californios and the "estranjeros," or foreigners.

Mission Santa Cruz was secularized in 1834 and an attempt was made to turn over some of its land to the remaining Indians. A quake in 1840 shattered the church and by 1846 so little remained of the mission that even Governor Pio Pico couldn't find anything left to sell.

Another earthquake in 1857 tumbled the front wall and the rest collapsed during the next weeks of aftershocks. Mission Santa Cruz ceased to exist.

A half-scale replica of the mission church stands in Santa Cruz not far from the site of the original. Used for weddings and private services, it was built in 1931 and donated to the church by Mrs. Gladys Sullivan Doyle. All that is left of the original mission is a portion of the soldier's quarters nearby and some stone foundations at the rear of the modern church.

And about all that remains of Branciforte - where the city of Santa Cruz now stands - is Branciforte Avenue, originally laid out as the community racetrack by the residents of the ill-fated pueblo.

Nuestra Senora de La Soledad

Mission Nuestra Senora de la Soledad

Thirteenth in the chain of California missions, Mission Nuestra Senora de la Soledad seemed to get all the bad luck that traditionally goes with that number.

La Soledad was the right name for this mission. It was founded in solitude and perished in neglect. Both adobe walls and human beings can be worn down in the chill, wet winters and searing summers, but the mission served early Californians as a major resting place on El Camino Real.

Father Junipero Serra, returning to Monterey after having founded Mission San Antonio, camped there in July 1771. He named the site "Soledad" because an Indian woman answered his questions with a single word sounding like the Spanish word for solitude.

On October 9, 1791, Father Fermin de Lasuen - successor to Father Serra - raised a great wooden cross and formally founded Mission Soledad. It was to administer to Indians of the area and close the 78-mile gap between Carmel and Mission San Antonio.

In fact, Soledad is in pleasant surroundings in a fertile valley bordered by rolling hills and distant mountains. Mission Soledad and its padres did, however, lead a hardscrabble existence. As at Santa Cruz, founded two weeks earlier, there were no mission goods or furnishings for Soledad, so essential articles had to be donated by existing missions. Fathers Diego Garcia and Mariano Rubi converted only 14 Indians in the first four months. The brushwood shelters built in 1791 were not replaced by an adobe church until six years later.

Father Garcia's place was taken shortly by Father Bartolome Gili, so that Soledad was briefly under the charge of two unconventional priests who had scandalized the Franciscan College of San Fernando in Mexico City only a few years earlier. Escapades such as slipping out of the college at night and rolling bowling balls down the dormitory halls after midnight earned them assignment to distant Alta California.

There, wrote Father Lasuen, they were "always grumbling, always restless, agreeing with no one and not even each other." Father Rubi was sent back to Mexico for medical care in 1793. The following year Father Gili, to everyone's relief, was authorized to take a ship for Baja California. The ship carried him instead to the Philippines, and Father Gili passed from the pages of California history.

The Indian population grew slowly. An epidemic killed many in 1802 and frightened away the others for a while. The mission's peak was in 1805, when there were 688 converts there - one of the smallest numbers of neophytes in the mission chain.

Nevertheless an extensive irrigation system was constructed so that crops flourished despite the rainless summers. Great herds of cattle were built up through the years so that the mission, lonely and unimpressive as it was, still managed to contribute substantial support to the civil government as well as care for the physical and spiritual needs of the neophytes.

Men broke down quickly at La Soledad. One of those to survive the longest was Father Florencio Ibanez, who lasted 15 years before he died at 78 in 1818. He was buried at the mission beside the grave of an old friend, Governor Jose Arrillaga. One of the few governors who gave complete support to the Franciscans, Arrillaga helped build "the golden age" of the missions.

There was not much new building activity at Soledad, because the missionaries were hard-pressed to keep the older buildings in repair. The church was badly damaged by a flood in 1828 and the next year Alfred Robinson called the mission the gloomiest, bleakest, most abject-looking spot in all California." In 1832 Father-Prefect Vicente Sarria reported that a small chapel had been erected to replace the ruined adobe church.

Father Sarria had come to the declining mission himself in 1828 when he was unable to staff it with anyone else. The College of San Fernando could send him no more missionaries, but he managed to keep the mission going himself. In 1835, the year after the mission the mission was secularized, Father Sarria succumbed to the rigors of his lonely post, unattended by a brother Franciscan. Neophytes carried his remains to Mission San Antonio for burial.

Thus Soledad ceased to exist as an operating mission. The land and its crumbling buildings were sold by Governor Pico for $800 to Feliciano Soberanes in 1846.

Until recent years, Mission Soledad consisted only of a few sections of adobe walls nearly buried by the tall grasses. In 1954 restoration of the chapel was started by the Native Daughters of the Golden West and in 1961-62 the west wing of the compound was restored. Of the church - only the outlines of its foundation, a few floor tiles and boards outlining the graves of Father Ibanez and Governor Arrillaga remain.

However, the parishioners of Soledad and the rest of the townspeople hold an annual fiesta to raise funds for the completion of the restoration work. Some day, La Soledad will stand again as it did in its prime - surrounded still by the green farms of the Salinas Valley.

San Jose de Guadalupe

Mission San Jose de Gualalupe

Large Palm Trees stand over Mission San Jose, as if to protect all that remains of what was once a giant among missions. Built on the crossroads of history, San Jose achieved greatness early in life; through its dusty plaza strode the priests and adventurers of legend.

There were 13 missions existing in 1795 when Father-Presidents Lasuen determined to close the gaps in the chain with five new missions. The site for the first of them-La Mission del Gloriosissimo Patriarca San Jose - was to be near the southeastern shore of San Francisco Bay, suitable distant from the pueblo of San Jose.

In a driving rainstorm in November of 1795, a survey party erected a cross where the mission was to be and galloped back to the shelter of Mission Santa Clara. On June 11, 1797, Father Lasuen dedicated the mission and soldiers and Indians started work on the temporary shelters, chapel and the stockade. Cattle from other missions were driven there, the nucleus of great herds that would graze at San Jose and its outlying ranchos.

Because the mission sat astride a main route into the San Joaquin Valley, it ministered not only to local Indians but to neophytes attracted from the interior, where many hostile tribes roamed. Thus the padres got caught up in conflict - accompanying military groups against marauding tribesmen or riding into hostile camps to persuade runaway neophytes to return. In 1805, Father Pedro de la Cueva ventured into the valley to care for some sick neophytes, fell into an ambush and escaped with his life only because he got away in a thick tule fog.

International affairs touched the growing mission early. On April 8, 1806, Count Nikolai Rezanof sailed into San Francisco Bay aboard the tiny Russian ship Juno, seeking supplies for starving colonists at Sitka, Alaska. The padres furnished corn, flour and beef in return for cloth and staged a fiesta in honor of one of Rezanof's aides.

That same year one of the great figures in the history of the Franciscan missions, Father Narcisco Duran, arrived to take over the direction of Mission San Jose. He found the adobe walls of a permanent church beginning to rise and Indians were dragging great redwood beams from the hills to the north. Of plain and undistinguished architecture, the new church was completed in 1809.

Father Duran took advantage of almost two decades of relative peace to expand the mission into a large and prosperous settlement. A gifted musician, he developed an impressive orchestra and chorus among the Indian converts. In 1825 he became president of the missions.

Four white men in ragged buckskins and several Indians rode into the plaza at Mission San Jose on August 22, 1827. Their 25-year-old leader was Jedediah Smith, American trapper, mountain man and explorer - already a legend in his own time. Father Duran greeted him coldly, for Mexican authorities had a warrant for his arrest. Also, a recent mass desertion of 400 San Jose neophytes was attributed (wrongfully) to the workings of the Yankee who had been camping in the interior.

Young Smith managed to clear himself with the Californians. He stayed at the mission to outfit his group before moving on into Oregon - and into an Indian ambush in which most of his men were slain. Ewing Young and Kit Carson also outfitted at the mission.

A grim chapter in the history of Mission San Jose was the story of Estanislao - or Stanislaus - a gifted Indian leader and favorite of Father Duran who, in 1829, turned against his mentor and led an uprising in the San Joaquin Valley. He turned back two military groups which tried to assault his fortress in the woods beside what is now the Stanislaus River. A third group, under the command of then-Lt. Mariano Vallejo and Lt. Jose Sanchez, succeeded in defeating the renegades in a three-day running battle. Estanislao escaped, but many Indians were killed and the soldiers executed a number of prisoners on the spot.

Father Duran protested the brutality and later forgave Estanislao, who returned to the mission where he died of smallpox 10 years later. In 1833 Father Duran turned the mission over to the Zacatecan order of Franciscans and moved his headquarters to Santa Barbara. The mission was secularized the following year but managed to survive until it was sold for $12,000 by Governor Pico in 1846.

The sale was promptly annulled by the United States which acquired California from Mexico the following year. The mission continued to function, but in 1868 the great adobe church was destroyed by a violent earthquake. A wooden Gothic church was built the following year and still serves the community.

Restoration of the only remaining adobe structure, part of the priests' living quarters, was finished in 1915 and 1916. That, and a grove of olive trees planted by the padres and the Indians, are all that remains of one of the most notable missions in the Franciscan chain.

San Juan Bautista

Mission San Juan Bautista

Rising like an island in the relentless river of time is Mission San Juan Bautista. Never a noble or neglected ruin, its buildings appear today much as they did more than a century ago when Mexican soldiers drilled on the plaza in front of the mission.

For many years, from 1812 when the mission was completed until about the end of the Civil War, the building had no bell tower. The Padre who had the steeple built hired carpenters who produced a wooden steeple that was much like those found in New England. The building was remodeled on other occasions, but was returned to its original appearance in 1949.

On two other sides of the grassy square are many of the town's original buildings - furnished, from bar to bedrooms, just as they were in yesteryear. The fourth side of the plaza overlooks the fertile fields of the San Benito River valley, little changed in appearance from the pastoral days of the padres.

Of the 21 California missions in the Franciscan chain, Father Junipero Serra founded the first nine. His successor, Father Fermin de Lasuen, established an equal number, of which San Juan Bautista was sixth. It was dedicated on June 24, 1797 - only 13 days after Father Lasuen founded Mission San Jose.

California Missions

Within six months, San Juan had a solidly-built chapel of wood and adobe and quarters for its two priests; before the year was out there were regular barracks for the soldiers, a big kitchen, houses for the neophytes, a guardhouse and granary.

Although the mission was built east of the original route of El Camino Real, the road soon curved past San Juan because of its prosperity and strategic setting. It stood as a buffer between the coastal settlements and the often warlike Tulare Indians of the interior.

Indian trouble flared intermittently through the years. One night in 1798 Indians surrounded the mission but were persuaded to leave peaceably. The following year, however, an Indian raid resulted in the death of eight neophytes. Severe reprisals by the Spanish soldiers caused peace for a while but mission lore says that raids by the Tulare Indians stopped the longest when Father Arroyo de la Cuesta won them over with a concert on a barrel organ.

It was Father de la Cuesta - architect, scholar, musician, linguist and man of many enthusiasms -who gave the present church a design unusual among the mission chapels. Work on the church had started in 1803, and when he arrived at San Juan in 1808 he expanded the structure to include two additional naves, one on either side of the altar. Unfortunately, by the time the church was completed in 1812, the Indian population had fallen off sharply and the great church was too big for the congregation. The big arches leading to the naves were bricked up and though Father de la Cuesta succeeded in increasing the congregation considerably, the church was never restored to its original form.

Gradually a small village grew up around the mission. An adobe barracks for soldiers was built on the plaza in 1814-15 and this became the Plaza Hotel - a famous stage stop in later years. Jose Castro built a two-story house on the plaza in 1825 and this became the headquarters for his successful revolt against Governor Gutierrez in 1836. It was Castro who rallied Mexican troops against Lt. John C. Fremont when, in March of 1846, the brash American's "survey party" invaded the valley. Driven off nearby Gabilan Peak,

Fremont was back at San Juan in July to raise the American flag - a state of war with Mexico having been proclaimed by President Polk on May 13.

In its heyday, Mission San Juan Bautista conducted a flourishing trade with Yankee ships at Monterey, bartering hides and tallow for goods and machinery. After secularization in 1834, the mission orchards and gardens were neglected as the neophytes gradually drifted back to their tribal lands. Yet never was San Juan without a priest, and even Governor Pio Pico stopped short of selling the church and friary when, in 1846, he was auctioning off mission properties as fast as he could.

A wooden bell tower was added in 1867 by Father Ciprian Rubio, the parish priest, so he could ring the bells from his bedroom in the tower. This jarring bit of architecture was later removed during restoration of the mission, which began with a fiesta on St. John's Day in 1907.

San Juan became an important stage stop during the Gold Rush and the little town was a beehive of activity. Then in the 1870's it was bypassed by the railroad and became again a rural town. In 1935 the plaza and the buildings around it except the mission which is now operated by Monterey diocesan priests were acquired by the state and converted into a State Historical Park. Today the mission church - still in use and former friary, a livery stable with a wonderful collection of horse-drawn vehicles, the old Plaza Hotel, the Castro Adobe and the Zanetta House all provide an authentic study of life in early California.

San Miguel Arcangel

Mission San Miguel Arcangel

A small brass cannon stands in the courtyard of San Miguel Arcangel, a reminder of the violence which so often intruded into the pious and peaceful compounds of the early California missions.

San Miguel's story begins on a searing July afternoon in 1797. In a little more than one month's time, Father-Presidente Lasuen had already founded two missions - San Jose and San Juan Bautista. Now he and his small party were on the banks of the Salinas River to establish yet another, San Miguel, to close the gap between Missions San Antonio and San Luis Obispo.

The start of Mission San Miguel was auspicious. A large crowd of Indians gathered to hear Father Lasuen dedicate the mission on July 25, 1797. And at the conclusion of the ceremonies, 15 Indian children were brought forward for baptism.

Father Buenaventura Sitjar from Mission San Antonio was placed in charge. Perhaps because he spoke the Indian language fluently the earliest years of the mission went relatively smoothly and buildings rose rapidly. But there were troubles.

Summer days were hot enough to wear a man down and,

indeed, Father Sitjar's assistant went insane. There were ants and termites and droughts that withered the wheat. The great bell of the mission cracked and became useless. In 1801, three padres were stricken with stomach pains and one died - poisoned, investigation proved, by drinking mescal from a tin and copper container.

By the end of the first year a large palisade had been erected, as well as a big adobe house and a chapel. The following year the chapel was replaced with a larger church and more houses were built. An elaborate irrigation system was developed to bring water from the river and building continued steadily in the early years. Then in August 1806, disaster struck.

A fire burned down two rows of houses, consumed half the roof of the church and destroyed so much food and supplies that he mission would have starved were it not for emergency help from other missions. Rebuilding began at once and by year's end the red tiled structures were more numerous than ever.

Father Juan Martin for 20 years was the great builder at San Miguel, developing a tannery, soap works, gristmill and granary, carpenter shop, a weaving room and a large roof-tile works. In 1810 buildings were erected at San Simeon to serve workers at the mission's coastal rancho. That same year, workmen began making adobe bricks for the construction of the present church.

Work on the church commenced in 1816. Neophytes had to cut and haul great timbers for the roof beams from pine forests at Cambria, 40 miles away. The church was finished in 1818. In 1823, artist Esteban Munras directed the Indians in frescoing and painting the interior which is as radiant today as it was about a century and a half ago.

But even as the church was completed, the mission's future darkened. Father Martin had long urged that a mission be built in the San Joaquin Valley. Father Juan Cabot had even selected a mission site on the Kings River, but the waves of revolution in Mexico eroded financial support for California missions.

On September 27, 1821, Spain's long rule of Mexico ended and Mexican administrators moved to secularize the missions. San

Miguel, with its prosperous ranchos, vast wheat fields and vineyards and thousands of head of cattle, was a tempting prize but it was not until late in 1834 that it was secularized. By 1841 there was only one white man (Father Ramon Abella) and 30 Indians living at the mission. The following year Father Miguel Gomez of San Luis Obispo took over the ministry of both missions and in 1846 Governor Pio Pico sold - illegally - what was left of San Miguel to Petronillo Rios and William Reed for $600. It was the last mission to be sold and the act set the stage for a grisly episode in California history.

Reed had visited the gold fields and had brought back some gold dust in 1848. He had also sold some cattle and sheep. In December of that year five deserters from a British man-of-war had dinner with the Reeds and heard references to his good fortune. They left, but slipped back at night to murder Reed, his wife and children and servants and visitors - eleven persons in all. They ransacked the mission in a futile search for gold and fled southward. A posse intercepted them near Santa Barbara. One was shot, one jumped into the ocean and was drowned and the other three were hanged. For years there were legends of ghosts prowling the ruins at the mission.

Following this tragedy, parts of the mission were rented for a saloon, a sewing machine agency headquarters, dance hall, store, warehouse, and living quarters. The church was without a priest and an aged Indian neophyte for years acted as an unpaid caretaker at the crumbling mission. He died, the story goes, while ringing the Angelus one evening. The bells remained mute until 1878 when a priest was again assigned to the mission.

Preservation and restoration activities took place through the years, but it was not until 1928 when the mission was returned to the Franciscans that a decade of extensive restoration work began. Today the mission stands remarkably well preserved, its church once again a place of worship and its grounds and buildings still an attraction for travelers.

San Fernando Rey de Espana

Mission San Fernando Rey de Espana

Majestic as its name, Mission San Fernando Rey de Espana today remains as one of the most inviting of all the missions in California. Ancient trees shade its cream-colored buildings; fountains and murmuring streams cool its gardens. Now surrounded by a metropolis, Mission San Fernando is as much an oasis today as it was when it stood alone on a treeless plain.

From its inception, the 17th mission in the Franciscan chain became a hub around which many great events turned. Battles were fought over the mission, treaties were signed on its grounds and the first gold rush in California took place close by.

Later, plundered and looted, its gardens turned into a hog farm, the mission was rescued from oblivion by Charles Lummis and the Landmarks Club.

The mission was founded on September 8, 1797, by the aged Father-Presidente Fermin de Lasuen. It was built to provide a resting place for travelers between San Gabriel and San Buenaventura missions and to minister to the large Indian population in the Encino Valley.

The site had been selected two years earlier - on the rancho of Francisco Reyes, Alcalde of Los Angeles. Reyes was given a much larger rancho in exchange. The mission was successful immediately. On the day of its founding, 10 Indian children were brought forward for baptism; two months later a small church had been completed and 40 neophytes were living at the mission. In 1799 a second and larger church was completed and buildings forming the traditional quadrangle were well along. In 1804 work was begun on the present church, which was completed in 1806.

By that time the mission was producing hides, soap, tallow, cloth and other products in considerable quantities. Travelers in increasing numbers were stopping at the mission and the padres' quarters were constantly being enlarged to accommodate these visitors. At the end of 13 years the building reached a length of 243 feet - today the largest original structure remaining in the mission chain. Its reception room was like a hotel lobby, but visitors were housed and fed for as long as they wanted to stay with no payment asked.

Beginning in 1810, increasing difficulties also visited the padres of San Fernando. The Hidalgo Revolution in Mexico forced Spain to cut off funds for the military in California, so that much of what was produced at San Fernando was requisitioned to support the idle soldiery. The resentful Indians began drifting away, their departure often hastened by harassment from the settlers who coveted their land. The padres struggled valiantly to preserve their lands and Indian community - for the fleshpots of Los Angeles and Santa Barbara corrupted many a neophyte.

In 1822 the flag of Mexico was raised in California and San Fernando's troubles increased. In 1834 the mission was secularized and the following year Father Francisco Ibarra - unable to witness the degradation of his mission and his beloved Indians - deserted his post and fled to Sonora, Mexico. It was a breach of trust which even Father-Presidente Narcisco Duran could not fault him for, and he was permitted to resume his post when he returned a year later in the vain hope that things would improve.

A group of young Californians, seeking mission lands, led a series of revolts and uprisings that swirled around the missions. Governor Jose Maria Echeandia, who decreed the secularizing of the missions in 1831, was deposed by the Mexican government. With the aid of the rebels however, he defeated the forces of his successor, Manuel Victoria, in a comic-opera battle at Cahuenga Pass on Mission San Fernando land.

The lure of mission lands grew even stronger in 1842 when gold was discovered close to San Fernando, the ensuing gold rush adding to the padre's troubles.

In 1845 another governor, Manuel Micheltorena, tried to aid the missions but he, too, was defeated in a "battle" at Cahuenga Pass. The victor, Pio Pico, became interim governor and launched a program to parcel out all that was left of the missions. Of San Fernando, there was but very little - but he leased it to his brother, Andres, for $1,120 a year, later selling the mission entirely.

Capt. John C. Fremont camped at San Fernando in January 1847 before moving on to Cahuenga Pass to accept the surrender of the forces of Andres Pico. California fell firmly into American hands. Although much of the mission land was returned to the church in a decree signed by Abraham Lincoln in 1862, the mission itself fell on increasingly hard times.

It was used as a warehouse and stable, its gardens became pigsties, its roof tiles were taken for other buildings and the floor of the great church was dug up by persons foolishly seeking buried treasure.

In 1896 the Landmarks Club launched a campaign to restore the magnificent buildings and the fortunes of San Fernando began to improve. In 1923 the church returned to the mission and placed it in the hands of the Oblate Fathers. Today its gardens and much of the quadrangle have been restored and the "long building" houses a rich assortment of relics.

San Luis Rey de Francia

Mission San Luis Rey de Francia

Largest and most prosperous of any mission in the Americas was San Luis Rey de Francia. Built on a hill east of present-day Oceanside, the mission dominated much of the economic life of early Southern California.

The site was selected by Father-Presidente Fermin de Lasuen, who dedicated the mission on June 13, 1798. It was the ninth and last to be founded by Lasuen and brought to 18 the number of missions that stretched in a chain from San Diego to San Francisco - most of them only a day's journey apart.

All but the five most recently-founded missions were busy settlements with fine adobe or stone churches, workshops and extensive living quarters. Livestock grazed over almost a million acres, fruits and produce were being harvested from cultivated bottomlands and thousands of Indians were beginning to accept the benefits (and rigors) of civilization. It had been only 29 years since Father Junipero Serra had founded the first mission in the then-remote wilderness of Alta California.

When Father Lasuen rode off after dedicating Mission San

Luis Rey, he left behind two priests, a handful of soldiers, a two-room brush hut, a stock of church goods and a scanty collection of tools and materials consisting mostly of some pickaxes, a dozen plowshares, six crowbars, some blankets and two dozen bolts of cloth with which to clothe the naked Indians. From this meager beginning, the mission grew rapidly under the inspired direction of Father Antonio Peyri.

By 1802 the first adobe church had been replaced by a much larger one and in 1804 the traditional quadrangle had been completed. Building on a heroic scale, Father Peyri developed elaborate mission gardens and a lavanderia where Indian women bathed and washed their clothes in pools of charcoal-filtered water.

The present great church was started in 1811 and completed in 1815. A big wooden dome rose over the sanctuary and this later was topped by a windowed cupola skylight. The beauty of the mission and its gardens, the size of its fields and herds and the zeal of its missionaries drew large numbers of converts.

Father Peyri cooperated eagerly with officials after Mexico gained her independence. But he was rapidly disillusioned by the mounting attacks made by the government on the mission system and by the campaigns to lure Indians from the missions with promises of "freedom." Without any way of earning a living, the Indians surrendered their lands to settlers in exchange for food or whiskey while the mission fields slowly grew to weeds for lack of workers.

Unable to face the ruin of the mission which had been labored over for more than thirty years, and hoping to get help in Mexico City, Father Peyri slipped away one night in 1832 and headed for San Diego harbor. The next morning five hundred Indians, finding him gone, and guessing his intentions, followed him and pleaded with him to return. But the old priest, tears coursing down his cheeks, left on his vain quest.

He could do little in Mexico City and sailed off to Spain to retire to his homeland. He died eventually in Rome, still sorrowing over his beloved Indians who were, indeed, faring badly.

By 1842 there were only about 600 Indians at San Luis Rey

and at its asistencias. Many thousands of head of cattle had been slaughtered for hides. The missionaries bartered these with Yankee trading ships for goods they needed to keep the mission going. The mission's extensive vineyards were neglected and a succession of civil administrators had laid waste to its once-vaunted prosperity. Finally, in 1846, Governor Pio Pico - who had been fired as administrator of San Luis Rey a few years earlier - sold what was left of the mission he had plundered to his brother, Jose, and to another man for $2,437. The "King of the Missions" soon stood empty.

It was reoccupied by American soldiers during and after the war with Mexico and was the headquarters of the famed Mormon Battalion which had blazed the first wagon road to California in 1846-47. The mission and some of its lands were eventually returned to the church by the United States, but the desolation was so vast that there was little hope of restoration.

Then in 1893 San Luis Rey came to life again as a novitiate for the Zacatecan Franciscans of Mexico. More than half a century of restoration work began and today the mission exhibits much of its original grandeur. It is now used for cultural and ecumenical purposes and is a parish in the Diocese of San Diego.

Farther up the valley is the mission's old asistencia at Pala, built by Father Peyri in 1816. Restored in this century, Pala still ministers to the Indians whose land had been taken from them after the missions were secularized and who to this day are still eking out a living in the rocky hills to which they were relegated by the American government.

Santa Ines

Mission Santa Ines

Last to be rebuilt of the southern missions, Santa Ines had a turbulent history completely out of keeping with its pleasant setting in the beautiful valley of the Santa Ynez River. War, Indian raids, pirates and earthquakes beset the mission's inhabitants.

A hint of the mission's troubled future was given when Father-Presidente Estevan Tapis asked for a larger than normal guard when he left Santa Barbara to found the mission. The local Indians - the Chumash - were friendly but quick to affront, and the fierce Tulare tribes were frequent invaders.

Yet when Padre Tapis raised the traditional great cross and dedicated the mission on September 17, 1804, there were some 200 natives watching and 27 Indian children were brought forward to be baptized.

By the end of the year, an adobe church - roofed with poles and thatch - was in use and the first wing of the traditional mission quadrangle had been built.

By the end of 1812 the extensive mission buildings, their white walls and red-tiled roofs gleaming in the sun, dominated farmlands in the fertile valley. But on December 21, 1812, a great earthquake reduced the church and many of the buildings to piles of rubble and the agonizing task of rebuilding began.

Father Javier de Uria is credited with the design of the new church which, with its adjoining bell tower, was dedicated on July 4, 1817. Although the Indian population was never great (deaths about kept pace with baptisms), Mission Santa Ines enjoyed a period of relative prosperity.

When in 1818, the raiders of Argentine privateer Hippolyte Bouchard stormed ashore at Refugio Beach, Mission Santa Ines reaped an unexpected benefit. The Californians captured three of Bouchard's men - among them Joseph Chapman, a Boston sailor who claimed he'd been shanghaied by Bouchard. "Pirate Joe" was sentenced to be executed but his life was spared, according to legend, by the pleadings of the young daughter of Don Ortega whose ranch he had pillaged.

Paroled to the mission Chapman later designed and built the gristmill and adjoining reservoirs, the ruins of which are still visible. Guadalupe Ortega, the rancher's daughter, broke her arm and "Pirate Joe" set it skillfully. The grateful rancher offered Chapman anything he wanted and he chose the senorita. They were married at the mission in 1822. Don Jose Chapman soon became an influential figure in early California.

But troubles were brewing below the placid surface of mission life. Mexico gained her independence in 1821 and the missions, which had been supporting the soldiery since 1810, faced new levies. Between 1822 and 1827 the small mission at Santa Ines supplied the garrison at Santa Barbara with more than $10,000 in goods and supplies - for which it received worthless drafts on the Mexican treasury.

Indian resentment at this burden of supporting the idle soldiers burst into flame when a guard at Santa Ines flogged a neophyte. In a hastily planned revolt, the Indians attacked the mission (and also revolted at Missions Santa Barbara and La Purisima) on February 21, 1824. They put the shops and soldiers' quarters to the torch, but when the church caught fire they helped beat out the flames before fleeing to the interior.

In 1836 the mission was turned over to a civil administrator and it declined rapidly. The Indians gradually fled the mission, only half of which was retained by the padres. Lands went untilled and cattle were slaughtered to support the mission. Complete ruin was averted during the brief administration of a friendly governor, Manuel Micheltorena, who in 1843 returned almost 36,000 acres of former mission lands to the Bishop of California for the purpose of founding a college that would be open to all who wanted to attend.

The College of Our Lady of Refuge was the first college in California. Opened at the mission in 1844, it was later moved to a nearby ranch and was operated by various religious orders until 1881.

The troops of John C. Fremont camped at the mission in December of 1846 and, to avoid an ambush, were guided over the mountains by William Foxen, who had acquired some of the mission property. In succeeding years, the church was never actually abandoned and the diocese tried to preserve the old buildings by having families live at the mission.

The first concerted effort to restore the mission buildings came in 1904 when Father Alexander Buckler arrived as parish priest. For 20 years he directed rebuilding while his niece repaired the remarkable collection of ancient vestments now on display in the mission museum. In 1924 the Capuchin Franciscans took over the mission and major reconstruction was undertaken in 1947-48 and again in 1953-54.

Today only 11 of the original 22 arches and less than half of the original buildings remain. Yet its pastoral setting and its authentic furnishings take the visitor back a hundred years and more.

San Rafael Arcangel

Mission San Rafael Arcangel

San Rafael was a mission that was never intended to be. Once the mission was established, its success hastened its downfall. And when it vanished, it disappeared so completely that no one is sure of what its buildings looked like.

In a lovely setting beside San Francisco Bay, sheltered from the wind and fog by towering Mt. Tamalpais, Mission San Rafael Arcangel started life on December 14, 1817, as a sanitarium. Weakened by white men's diseases and the chill weather, Indians at Mission Dolores in San Francisco had been dying in appalling numbers.

As an experiment, a group of ailing neophytes clutching their blankets against the cold, was rowed over to the Marin shore. A few weeks in the sun brought a surprising improvement and when Father Luis Gil - who had some medical knowledge - volunteered to run the proposed asistencia Father-Prefect Vicente Sarria moved quickly to establish it.

A simple long building was erected out of adobe for use as a hospital, storehouse, priests' quarters and chapel. When the church was erected in 1818, it had no bell tower and the traditional quadrangle of buildings was never started.

Under the ministrations of Father Gil, many ailing Indians - first from San Francisco and later from other missions - recovered. Converts from local tribes swelled the size of the asistencia. The missionaries envisioned it as a base for new missions at Petaluma and Suisun, while the military used San Rafael as a stopping point for groups sent to keep an eye on the Russian settlements at Bodega and Fort Ross.

After two years, Father Gil was succeeded by Father Juan Amoros whose energy and zeal built the asistencia into a thriving community. Spain's last great exploring group in California left San Rafael in October 1821 and headed up the Sacramento Valley to probe reports of Yankee intrusions. It returned battered and starving the next month after going as far north as perhaps Mt. Shasta and coming down the valleys of the Eel and Russian rivers.

San Rafael was raised to full mission status on October 19, 1822. It weathered a move to close it the following year and reached its peak of prosperity in 1828 when 1,140 neophytes were living there.

The fear of Indian attacks was always present. The Russian trader and navigator Otto von Kotzebue visited San Rafael in 1824 and reported seeing two sentries on the hills, each with a fire burning all during the night. In 1829 Indians did attack the mission, seeking to kill Father Amoros who had many times successfully ventured into their lands to win converts. They laid waste to much of the mission and stole horses and cattle, but the neophytes formed a human wall around their padre and hustled him to a safe hiding place.

The fortunes of Mission San Rafael changed for the worse in 1832 when Father Amoros died. The mission was transferred to the Zacatecan Franciscans and Father Jose Mercado was placed in charge. He came in conflict with General Mariano Vallejo, military comandante and neighboring land owner, who accused Father Mercado of ordering an attack of armed neophytes on some pagan Indians, 21 of whom were killed. The padre was summarily suspended from his post and held for ecclesiastical trial, but investigation proved him to be innocent and he was restored to duty. The mission was secularized in 1834 - the first of all the missions to be taken over - and Vallejo was appointed administrator.

In 1837 Vallejo took over Indian lands and livestock - for later distribution - on the grounds the property was being improperly used. Some was returned in 1840. In 1846 Governor Pio Pico sold the mission to his brother Andres and to Antonio Sunol for $8,000, a sale later ruled void by the Americans. The mission was abandoned in 1855 and its decaying building was sold by the church in 1861 to James Byers, a carpenter. Byers tore down all that was left to salvage including the valuable hand-hewn beams.

In 1869 St. Raphael's church was built on the mission site, a handsome Gothic edifice which burned down in 1919. By then the only relic of Mission San Rafael was a marker. In excavating for the foundations of the present church, workmen turned up old roof tiles and these were used for fill.

In 1949 a replica of the old mission was built with Hearst Foundation funds. The chapel was turned around to face the mountains instead of the bay and the star-shaped windows over the entrance may never have existed in the original church. Contemporary sketches of the old building vary markedly on such details. Even the sketch many historians deem most authentic was made from memory by General Vallejo, when he was in his 70's.

San Francisco Solano

Mission San Francisco Solano

The remarkable mission system which Father Junipero Serra had planted in the wilderness a half century earlier was entering its twilight years when Mission San Francisco Solano was founded in 1823.

Mexico had gained its independence and the aging Spanish-born padres in California would have been deported except for the fact there was no one to take their place. Settlers were moving onto mission and Indian lands. The soldiers had not been paid for years and openly talked of throwing their support behind any foreign power that would pay their back wages.

Rival politicians struggled for supremacy, while in the crumbling Mission San Buenaventura Father-Presidente Jose Senan lay dying.

In San Francisco, Father Jose Altamira noted in despair that there were only about fifty able-bodied Indian neophytes surviving, women were doing men's work "and the mission cannot subsist this way." Without consulting Senan, he proposed to Governor Luis Arguello that Mission Dolores and its sister mission, San Rafael, be closed and their functions combined into a new mission to be founded in the pleasant valley of Sonoma.

The governor and the legislature in Monterey agreed, seeing this as a way of interposing another settlement between the Russians at Fort Ross and the rest of California. So it was that on July 4, 1823, Father Altamira raised a cross at Sonoma and transferred the name of San Francisco to the new mission. Only upon his return to "old" San Francisco did he notify his superiors of what he had done.

Shocked by this breach of discipline and by the political interference in mission affairs, Father Vicente Sarria, Senan's successor, nevertheless agreed to a compromise. Missions San Francisco de Asis ("Dolores") and San Rafael Arcangel would remain, and Father Altamira could proceed at Sonoma, but the mission would he called San Francisco Solano.

A crude wooden building, covered inside and out with whitewashed mud, was built and dedicated on April 4, 1824. A long adobe wing was next completed for living quarters and this structure is still standing. Cattle and neophytes came from Mission Dolores, while the Russians at Fort Ross unexpectedly donated many useful articles, including bells.

A vineyard, orchard and garden were planted. Tiles and adobe brick were manufactured and soap making and hide tanning were started. But Father Altamira was plagued by trouble with hostile Indians and runaway neophytes. Dejected, he bad himself transferred to San Buenaventura in 1826 and was succeeded by Father Fortuni, under whose guidance the mission soon reached a peak of prosperity.

A large adobe church was completed in 1833 to form most of the eastern side of the quadrangle of mission buildings. But by then the waves of change were beginning to erode this northernmost mission.

Concerned about the Russian settlement which had been on the California coast since 1812, Governor Jose Figueroa assigned Lt. Mariano Vallejo to colonize the area surrounding Bodega and

Fort Ross. He founded the pueblo of Sonoma in 1835, a year after the mission had been secularized, with Vallejo as chief administrator.

The inevitable conflict began. Father Jose Quijas threatened to leave unless Antonio Ortega, his worst tormentor, was fired as an administrator. But Ortega was elevated to mayordomo and Father Quijas served the mission, by then a parish church, from San Rafael.

The mission decayed so rapidly that in 1840 Vallejo built the present chapel, probably using bricks and timber from the old church. He added a wooden cupola on top during alterations in 1858-60.

In 1841 the Russians withdrew from Fort Ross, partly because they had trapped out all the sea otter and partly because of Vallejo's colonizing activities. But Sonoma was destined to feel the march of another empire. Vallejo declared for annexation of California to the United States, but the growing number of Americans in the area feared that Mexico planned to expel them. On June 14, 1846, a small band led by Ezekiel Merritt and William B. Ide seized Sonoma, made Vallejo a prisoner, and ran up a crude flag displaying a star and a grizzly bear.

For 23 days, California was an independent republic. Then on July 7, Commodore John Sloat seized Monterey and raised the American flag. Vallejo was released to play a major role in founding the state.

Mission Solano, however, fared badly. It was sold in 1881 and subsequently used as a barn, winery and blacksmith shop. The buildings were saved from disintegration when they were purchased by the Historic Landmarks League in 1903 and turned over to the state in 1906, just as the earthquake shattered the chapel.

Restoration work started in 1910 and has continued to this day. One of the first State Historical Monuments, the mission buildings are administered by the State Department of Parks and Recreation.

Epilog

The illustration of Mission San Carlos on the cover and the drawings previously mentioned are reproduced through the courtesy of the Bancroft Library, University of California, Berkeley. The illustrations of the missions in the 19th Century are from the collection of James Stevenson Publisher.

The model construction section which follows, displays the work of David Graham of Modesto, California. He has suggestions for construction of a model of a California Mission.

History & Model Building Ideas for Children

David Graham's Model Construction Guide

Mr. Graham constructed the models which you see here.

San Francisco Solano Mission

Santa Barbara Mission

Model Building Ideas for Children

Our thanks to Mr. Graham for his Mission model construction ideas using Styrofoam. He has carefully thought through some very successful methods, and offers a caution at the beginning. He writes, "Parents, it will be *very* difficult, if not impossible, to finish this project in less than 6 hours, and this does not include getting all of the materials together! You cannot work on the whole mission while parts are not dry, so plan to work on your model over several days or evenings. Also, your child needs your assistance. Do not, under any circumstances let the child cut Styrofoam or other pieces. You must cut those items yourself, using appropriate protection such as gloves."

You can use all the information about the missions you can find. The first part of this book contains a brief history of each mission, and the following section has a layout or diagram for each mission. Mr. Graham finds it very helpful to go to the mission, participate in the guided tours and demonstrations when available. Not only is it fun, but both parents and children learn a lot. While at the mission gather any printed material on that mission that may be available and take pictures. After the reading and research has been completed, you will want to gather the necessary materials and tools for construction. This guide has been developed to provide basic information for those of us who have never completed a project of this kind.

A Message to 4th Graders:

You will need to have an adult help you with this project. We will present the instructions for Styrofoam construction. No matter which model you make, your adult assistant should help you with shopping. On the next pages we list a few things you will need to buy.

Warning!

An adult must do all cutting of Styrofoam, using gloves to

protect hands, and using great care. When working with unfamiliar materials extra caution is necessary.

Be very careful during your model building, even though an adult is helping. You and your parent or other helping adult should read this guide together and talk about it before you start. If you read through all the suggestions before you start, you will save time. The materials needed to complete the project should be purchased as soon as you have read this book, selected your mission and looked at the layout. Remember, Please read everything which follows before you begin.

Parental Planning

As you read, make a list of things you will need to buy or to find. Set aside enough time to shop for the things you need. A Saturday afternoon shopping trip with your child is recommended, so that you can buy what is needed together. This hopefully will be a leisurely process. As you buy items, briefly explain how you intend to use them. Children will learn and will enjoy the process of creating a model if they understand what they are doing. Shorter work sessions of one-half hour or less are much better than working for hours at a time. By the time you are done they will have learned to plan - in addition to learning about a California Mission.

If your child leaves for any reason, bring them back to the project for a few minutes and stop together. Set easily attained goals and help your 4th grader fix errors. Two short work sessions in an afternoon or evening are much better than one very long session. Remember, it will be very difficult to finish this project in less than 6 or 7 hours. You certainly will not finish your model in one evening. Remember to find and praise the good in what your child has done. Be sure to help them realize this is *their* project.

So, how big a project do you want to take on? Deciding this is the most important step. Before getting the materials together to begin your mission construction project, you should decide how much of the mission grounds you want to create. Will you be building the church, a very good project by itself, or will you be building the church with the workshops, storage rooms and living quarters. As you consider this choice, think about how the model will be transported to the classroom and about what size project you can easily carry.

The first step, after you have selected the mission you will build, is to decide how big you will make the Mission Church. Find a picture or drawing of the mission church and look at how long workshops are compared to the church. By starting your planning with the size of the Mission Church, you can base the height and length of other buildings on the size of the main structure, the church. (If, for example the storage buildings are smaller than the church, estimate how much smaller and plan accordingly.)

Your "Blueprint" of the Model

A blueprint is a drawing used to help a builder decide how much space will be taken up when one builds a house or other building. To make your plan, follow this guide.

Once you have decided on the size of the project, you should get some newspaper and a felt tip pen - to create a rough layout so you will know where each building will be placed in your mission project. Cut the newspaper to the size of the Styrofoam base you will use - 24 inches wide by 48 inches long. If necessary, tape pieces of the newspaper together to match the size of the base.

Draw lightly as you make your outline of the church so that you can make changes if you decide to move things around a bit. You should save your drawing of the layout so that you can check the partially completed model buildings before fixing them on the base.

You will find that some of the mission churches had a rather unusual size and shape. They were sometimes very long and narrow. By doing the "blueprint" sketch first, you can avoid the frustration of having your layout not fit on the base as expected. It is not necessary to spend a great deal of time on the sketch, but whatever time it takes is well spent.

Collecting the building materials

Materials used by Mr. Graham are available from a home building supply or lumber supply store. For the base he purchases a 1 inch thick piece of white Styrofoam insulation material. This is available in 24 x 48 inch pieces. This is a standard size. For the walls and building construction he purchases a second piece of 3/4 inch thick Styrofoam, 24 inches x 48 inches. If available, the Styrofoam packing blocks that come with computers, stereo equipment or other appliances can sometimes be used to make buildings.

The tools needed are not too expensive. In fact you may have some of these items in a home workshop. Those things you need can be found at a local hardware store. Mr. Graham buys a 12 pound pail of sheet rock All-Purpose Joint Compound, a 4 inch and an 8 inch plastic putty knife and white all-purpose glue, like Elmer's Glue or the equivalent. At some of the large home improvement warehouses the 8 inch plastic putty knife cost $1.19 and the other knife was even less. At a supermarket he gets chocolate syrup for dying the joint compound paste which is spread on the base for the landscape. You will need to experiment with the colors to get the brown you want. (See additional mixing instructions in, "Beginning Construction" section.)

Your list of materials also includes gloves, a paint stirring stick, fine sand paper, sturdy tooth picks, fine point felt marker, ruler, electric knife or some other short knife to cut the Styrofoam, scissors, hacksaw blade and newspaper to cover your work area and some rags to wipe your hands on.

If your budget for this project is limited, some families may prefer more inexpensive building materials, free cardboard and packing containers like shoe boxes or milk cartons. The material you use for a base should be fairly rigid, but light enough for a parent or a 4th grader to carry. A light and thin plywood, fiber-

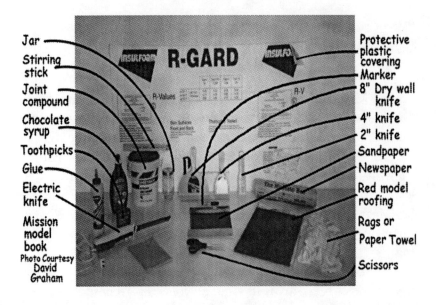

Jar
Stirring stick
Joint compound
Chocolate syrup
Toothpicks
Glue
Electric knife
Mission model book

R-GARD

Protective plastic covering
Marker
8" Dry wall knife
4" knife
2" knife
Sandpaper
Newspaper
Red model roofing
Rags or Paper Towel
Scissors

Photo Courtesy David Graham

works very well for the base, as well as for construction of the mission itself.

Beginning Construction

When you have the materials for the basic structure assembled, you are ready to start with cutting and assembly. One method of cutting is to use an electric knife, (one that you might use to cut a turkey) to cut out the pieces that you need. You must have an adult help with this process. Leather gloves should be worn to protect hands - always use safe working practices. Place some material under the Styrofoam to be sure that the surface on which you are working will not be damaged by the cutting process, as you cut the Styrofoam. This is important whether you use a regular knife or an electric knife as is suggested by Mr. Graham. Regardless of the knife you use, you may need to make several cuts along the same line to cut through the Styrofoam. After the pieces of the

Joining Building Walls

If 3/4 inch Styrofoam is used for your building walls, you can hold the walls together temporarily by using toothpicks. Holding a piece of Strofoam with one hand, push the toothpick far enough in so that it won't stick out of the other wall when the two pieces are pushed together. Then take the piece you want to join, and position it so that when the bottoms of the pieces are even. Then push the two pieces together so that they hold the corner of the building in place as you see in the diagram below.

When you are ready to glue the walls together, you can pull them apart about 1/2 inch, creating a space to join pieces. You can then apply glue to both surfaces, using a popsicle stick or something similar. Push the pieces back together and the toothpicks will help hold the two walls in the correct position while the glue dries.

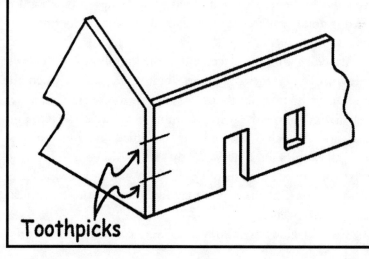

Toothpicks

walls are cut, put them together on your blueprint to make sure they fit and are to the scale that you want.

Do not cut all of the pieces at once, as you may need to trim and make buildings slightly smaller. Do only one building at a time. Doing the walls first allows you to see the space your church will occupy. When you feel that the size of the buildings and fence walls are correct, and fit nicely on your blueprint, you are almost ready to begin gluing.

If you want to have windows and doors of wood, we recommend that you cut the wood first - to the right size for the opening you are making - then trace the outline of the wooden window cover or door on the Styrofoam. Number your wood pieces starting with the front doors as the first piece. Set aside your doors and windows in order, and then cut out the openings where they will be placed. (See the upcoming section on cutting the thin wood window covers.)

Next, before you glue your buildings together fasten them together by pushing a couple of round, sturdy toothpicks into the Styrofoam. These toothpick will be buried in the pieces you are joining. You should use something hard, such as a thimble or leather gloves to push on the toothpicks so that you don't hurt your fingers. If the Styrofoam breaks, don't worry. You can glue it back together, and in 12 hours it will be as good as new. The bond is quite strong and the material can still be used in constructing your mission.

After checking the placement of the buildings and fields on the base, you can pull the edges apart slightly add glue and then put the building walls and ceilings together again with the glue in place. Mr. Graham recommends letting your model dry at least overnight. The next day, when all of the buildings are glued together, it is time to put together the solid fence walls that surround your fields. You probably won't need the toothpicks for this, as you glue the fence walls into sections, however you may like the way the toothpicks hold the pieces together.

After the glue has dried, you are ready to coat the buildings and fence wall segments with joint compound. You should stir the joint compound so that it is well mixed. Using your 4 inch putty knife, coat your exposed building walls and fence walls with the joint compound doing your best to get it as smooth as possible. A great thing about joint compound is that if you mess it up it can always be fixed. An area that is warm and dry is the best place to let the joint compound dry-this takes about 24 hours. If drying time is a concern, you might want to place the model in a dry warm location and use a fan to blow air over the model.

Always put the cover tightly on the bucket of joint compound, so that it doesn't dry out. After the joint compound has dried you can lightly sand it until it appears as smooth as you want it.

Now you will connect the buildings to the base. Before you do this, set aside some plain, uncolored joint compound in a jar with a lid. Close the jar tightly so that the compound doesn't dry out. This material may be used to do patches or repairs where necessary. To the rest of the joint compound add the chocolate syrup, a bit at a time, to get your joint compound to a light earthen brown color. Remember to add only a small amount of the color and to stir for 4 or 5 minutes to get it well mixed. It is usually better to have the earth be a bit light, rather than a bit dark. You might want to see what a sample looks like when it is dry before adding more if you think it is necessary. Many people add too much, and make the earth too dark. Very light brown, like the dusty hills and roads of summertime California is best.

Use the earth-colored joint compound mixture to completely coat the top and sides of the base using your 8 inch putty knife, spreading the material out as smooth as possible. This takes patience and a steady hand. Perhaps the parent can guide the application of small amounts to one section of the base by the 4th grader, and the parent can follow along spreading the material smoothly and carefully. Do not put out too much to spread evenly before it starts to dry. After the base is coasted to your satisfaction, you can carefully place your buildings and walls on it, pressing them down and working them into the base coating. You will also be gluing the fence wall sections together and to the buildings they may touch. After everything is in place let it dry for about two full days. Yes, two full days! It may be helpful to have the fourth grader mark the time on a calendar when the model can again be touched. You can then take the white joint compound that is in the jar and coat the places where you joined the pieces together, a small flat stick, like a paint stirrer works best for this.

Roofing, Windows and Doors

Sturdy windows and doors were necessary in the original missions, because of possible attack, and for light and ventilation. The adult who is helping can make some of the cuts for windows and for doors if you decide to add these.

For the windows and doors, Mr. Graham uses a saw to cut redwood or cedar strips. These are very thin pieces of wood that can be cut to the size of the windows and doors. If you can't cut your own pieces for doors, a package of cedar SHIMS about 15 inches long can be purchased at Home Deport or similar store or lumber yard. (Shims are used to fit a doorway and are basically shaped like a very slim wedge). One end of the shim is thin, about 1/8th of an inch think, and the other end is about 1/4th inch thick. You will cut off what you need with a very fine blade, like a hack saw blade. If you don't have a hacksaw, you can purchase an inexpensive hacksaw replacement blade, since that is all you need. These blades may vary a lot in price, you need only a very inexpensive one. (Hacksaws are usually used to cut metal. Yours will easily cut some soft, thin wood. Just wear your leather gloves to protect your hands as you cut off what you need.) If you glue the toothpicks to the doors, they can be stuck into the Styrofoam in an open position. If you want to glue them into place, they will be less likely to come loose and be lost.

The roofing material recommended by David Graham can be found at a hobby shop. It is made in plastic sheets and looks like

Roof Supports

If you have a long roof on your Church, you may have a sag in the roof line. You can put support under the roof of the Church, workshops or Padre's quarters by adding triagnular pieces of Styrofoam.

If you make the supports before you put the building together it is easy to trace the size of the end piece, see (A) below, so that the support, (B) below, is the same size and reaches from wall to wall.

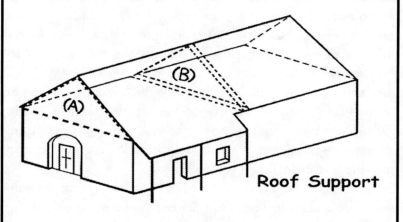

Roof Support

red tile roofing. This roofing material can sometimes be hard to find, and it is expensive, so you need to be careful how you lay it out so that you don't waste it. Mr. Graham says, "I like to cut the tile roofing material with a pair of scissors so that it just hangs over the edges of the building by about 1/4 to 1/2 inch. I also glue it on so both sides of a peaked roof meet at the top as close as possible. At the peak I cut a strip of the roofing material the long direction of the tiles, so it can be used to cover the ridge of the roof. In some cases I cut my roofing material so that it extends out to form a covered walkway in front of a building. When I do this, I cut small wood sticks for roof supports, which can be found lying on the ground in the park (redwood sticks are good if you can find them) or in your back yard. The roof must be supported with posts. The posts stand upright to hold the wood 'beams' which go under the roof for support." You might also use pieces of the shims as beams and posts.

For very long buildings, cut triangular pieces of Styrofoam to glue on top between the walls to help support the roofing material. If you can't find the plastic roofing material-or want to avoid the cost-try using the side or top of a cardboard box, with one side peeled away. It takes some time to reveal the little tile-like corrugated inner part of the box. You will need about 15 minutes to strip one six of a piece of cardboard to reveal the "tiles" inside. You can use a fingernail scissors to trim the loose paper from the "tiles," then you will need to paint them with a thick water color or other craft pain - color it a dark orange-red just like the mission tiles, perhaps more than one coat, to get the look you want. (A warning, *do not* **use spray paint in an aerosol can on Styrofoam.** It reacts with the Styrofoam and it will melt it.

Bells of about the right size can be made from drinking straws. To make a bell from this material, cut a new white or clear straw into 1/2 inch sections, then for each bell, pinch one end closed. Tape the pinched end so that it will stay closed, then get a piece of white or black plain cotton thread, (not nylon or fishing line because that is too stiff. The adult helping you should carefully push the needle through the plastic so that the bell can be hung in the campanile or bell wall using a staple or tack to secure the thread. Bells can also be purchased at a hobby shop.

If you are making a model of the entire mission grounds, you should look for materials in the neighborhood around you. A small twig could look like a fallen tree trunk. Pine twigs work well for small trees. Bits of sage brush or other materials may be good for fields.

Perhaps you could show some Indians at work hoeing, or a padre drawing water from a well. This will require some imagination on your part - both for the creation of the well and the making of figures. Clothing for figurines can be made of rags of white material and can be colored or left white. You will find that trial and error is the only way to get your model looking realistic. If you have little figures from toy sets you may want to use those for figures, or you may want to get some pipe cleaners and make your own figures. The pipe cleaner figures may work well with cloth cut and draped like a robe to look like a hooded Padre. Remember to keep the size of the figures roughly the right size for the buildings.

Be sure to complete your project several days ahead of time, so that paint and glue will have time to dry.

We have mentioned many materials. If you have drawn your layout, you will have decided how many buildings you are assembling. Most parents say that the un-rushed making of a model is one of the most enjoyable homework assignments that a parent and child can complete together. Have fun!

Diagrams of Mission Grounds

Mission layouts are in order of founding, starting with San Diego de Alcala and ending with San Francisco Solano. You many notice that the plans of the original missions show the layout of buildings that had collapsed by the time that Henry Chapman Ford drew the missions in the 1880's. (Compare illustrations in history section to layouts shown below.)

San Diego de Alcala Mission

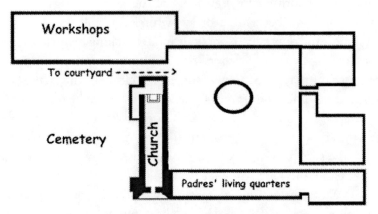

San Carlos Borromeo de Carmelo Mission

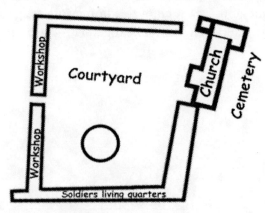

San Antonio de Padua Mission

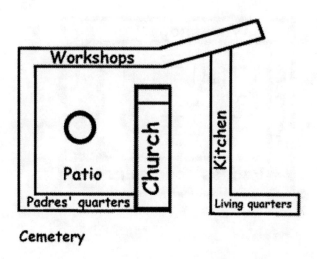

San Gabriel Arcangel Mission

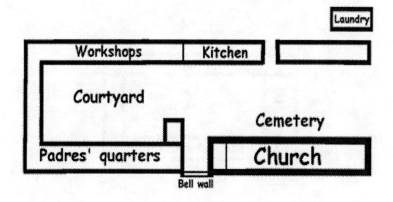

San Luis Obispo Mission

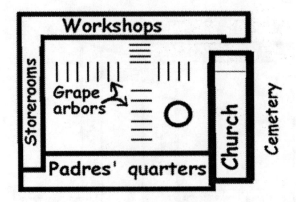

Saint Francis de Asis Mission

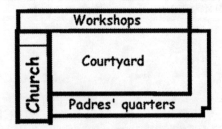

San Juan Capistrano Mission

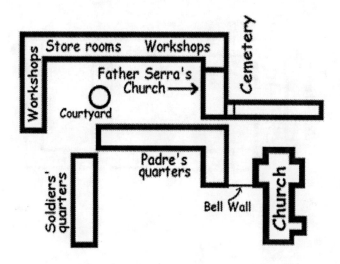

Santa Clara de Asis Mission

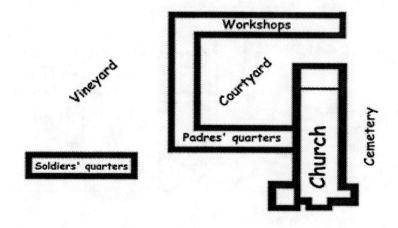

San Buenaventura Mission

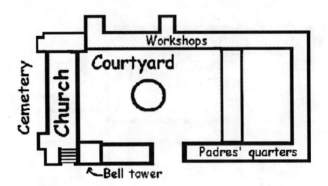

Santa Barbara Mission

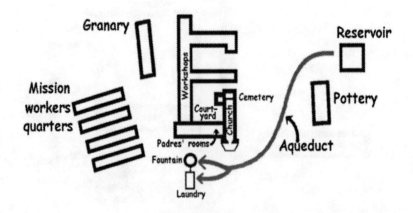

La Purisima Concepcion Mission

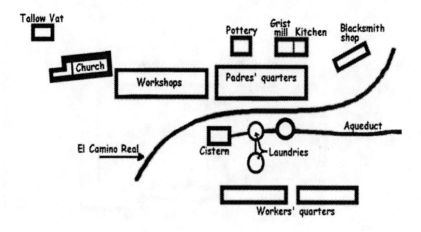

Santa Cruz Mission

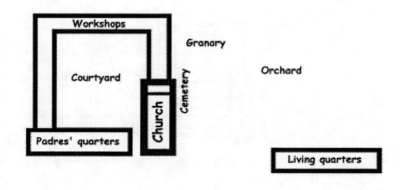

California Missions

Nuestra Senora de la Soledad Mission

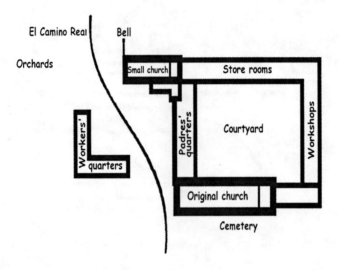

San Jose de Guadalupe Mission

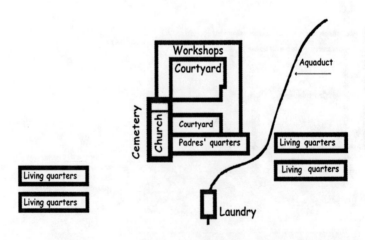

San Juan Bautista Mission

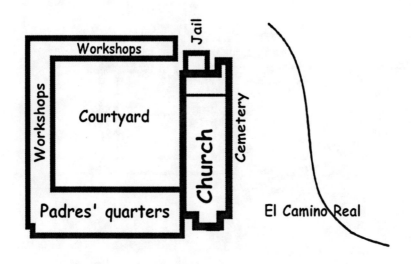

San Miguel Arcangel Mission

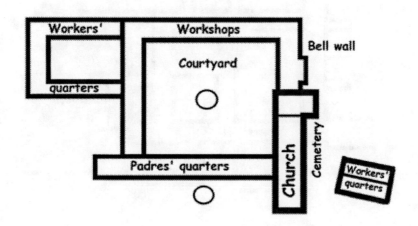

California Missions

San Fernando Rey de Espana Mission

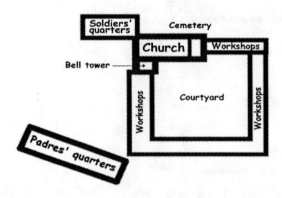

San Luis Rey de Francia Mission

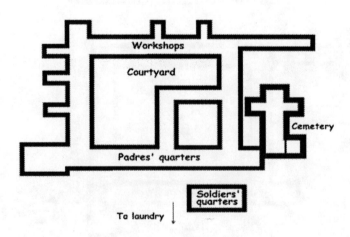

Santa Ines Mission

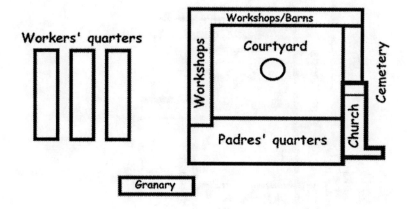

San Rafael Arcangel Mission

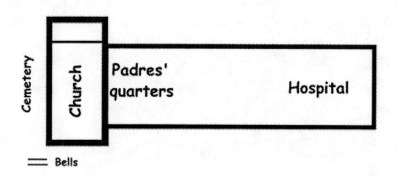

San Francisco Solano Mission

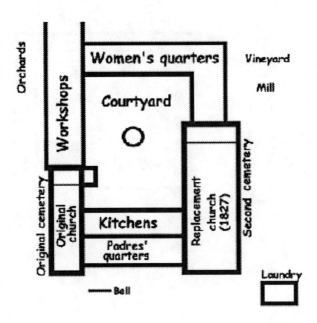

We welcome e-mail at jsp@jspub.com from readers. Please send us a photograph of your model made using Mr. Graham's suggestions, if you would like to have it printed in this book. We will select from the best models submitted and when we have one example for each mission we will produce an new edition of this book with the selected examples of readers' work.

California History books by
James Stevenson Publisher
1500 Oliver Road, Suite K-109
Fairfield, CA 94533
(707) 469-0237 or Fax (508) 374-7762

California History for Children
Nonfiction for children, parents, grandparents and
classroom teachers (from Cabrillo in 1542 to San Francisco
earthquake and fire in 1906)
Paperback, $8.95

I Love You, California - The California state song,
sung by Cathrael Hackler, with John Foster on Guitar
Great for classrooms
Audio tape, $7.95

(Robert Louis *)* Stevenson at Silverado*
Stevenson's honeymoon in California
Paperback, $10.95

Sam Brannan, Builder of San Francisco
(announced the Gold Rush to the world, started
Vigilance Committees)
Paperback biography, $13.95

The Capital That Couldn't Stay Put
Award winning non-fiction story of California's Capital
Paperback, $12.95

*Historical and Descriptive Sketchbook of
Napa, Sonoma, Lake and Mendocino, 1879*
The first history of what became the California wine country
Hardcover, $29.95

History of Alameda County, California, 1883
Major early history of this important county
Hardcover, 1000 pages, $39.95

LaVergne, TN USA
30 March 2010
177570LV00002B/117/A